GANGSTA

PARABLE OF A LOST SHEEP

BY: YVONNE REID

Copyright © 2024
YVONNE REID

All rights reserved. No part of this publication may be reproduced, copied, stored in a retrieval system, transmitted, scanned in any form or under any conditions, including, photocopying, electronic, recording, or otherwise, without the written permission of the author, Yvonne Reid.

978-1-998120-30-7 Published by:

COJ BOOKZ Toronto ONT

&

Restoration of the Breached without Borders
West Palm Beach, Florida 33407
restorativeauthor@gmail.com
Tele: (561) 388-2949

Cover Design aided by:
Leostone Morrison

Editor: Melisha Bartley Ankle

DEDICATION

To my children Tevon, Tushawn , Tumar, Tavisha and Tamika.

To my grandchildren Tristan, Trinity, Tamia, Emanuel, Nathaniel and Abraham David.

Sometimes I struggle wondering if I could have been a better mother. I didn't have it all put together but one thing I know was I will always love all of you.

ACKNOWLEDGEMENTS

To my mother Hyacinth Crowe who did her best to be a mother to me and my siblings.

Thank you to The Love Church (TLC) for all of your encouraging words to write this book.

I give God thanks for all the prophets and prophetess who prophesied about this book. I continue to pray into those prophetic words and watching the seeds grow into millions of fruits.

FOREWORD

She tells it all. The sharing of one's former dark truths have been stifled by the inability of the weak hearted to receive knowledge of realities that some cringes at. However, the impact of the forgiven continues to be remarkable. Yvonne Reid, formerly Gansta, has escaped the penitential incarceration of guilt and has beautifully penned her heart ripping truths. A very intriguing life which would easily be converted to a number one movie in the theatres. A life of migration, sex, drugs, guns, prison and near-death experiences, Yvonne unlike many, is alive to tell it all.

As I perused each page, my attention was gripped, and I intensely allowed each word to transport me into the unknown. I sincerely believe you will also be tremendously impacted and encouraged to not give up on anyone. Transformation is still possible. As seen with Yvonne formerly Gansta, she is transformed and renewed. As you delve into this work, be prepared to be challenged, inspired, and motivated to see the broken, lost and imprisoned be set free.

-Leostone Morrison (Author)
Mind Renewal: Biblical Secrets to A Better You
Cross Over, Etc

TABLE OF CONTENTS

Dedication	iii
Acknowledgements	iv
Foreword	v
Preface	viii
Chapter 1: Gangsta Style	1
Chapter 2: Childhood	4
Chapter 3: Adjusting to Canada	16
Chapter 4: Prophet Ezekiel	27
Chapter 5: New Friends	39
Chapter 6: The Runaway	52
Chapter 7: Death Threats	65
Chapter 8: The Return of Vace	77
Chapter 9: Getting Hooked	93
Chapter 10: Another Notch	104
Chapter 11: The Escape	123
Chapter 12: Are You Crazy?	139
Chapter 13: The Wild Ride	146
Chapter 14: Wanted	158

Chapter 15: The Idol   170

Chapter 16: Life Became Meaningless   180

Chapter 17: The Last Hurrah   192

Chapter 18: I Woke Up   208

Conclusion   212

About the Author   213

PREFACE

It took couple years for me to write this book and another couple of years to publish it. As I read through and edited, I realized that the missing pieces of the puzzles of my life was coming into place.

All the years of my life, I had many questions that I couldn't understand. The more I wrote, the more everything was being answered.

This book is intended to save lives, to help others to make better choices and to understand things that happened in their life was for a purpose. No matter what it was, whether good or bad.

It all went down for a reason and even though somethings we will never understand why. We would still have a choice to live with it or let it kill us.

Well, I choose to live with it and use it for the glory of God. My story can make you a better person.

MATHEW 18: 12-14

"If a man has a hundred sheep and one of them wanders away, what will he do? Won't he leave the ninety-nine others on the hills and go out to search for the one that is lost? And if he finds it, I tell you the truth, he will rejoice over it more than over the ninety-nine that didn't wander away! In the same way, it is not my heavenly Father's will that even one of these little ones should perish.

Chapter 1
Gangsta Style

"Miss Yvonne please, do not go to that dance." Lisa pleaded 'Only God can stop me from going" I responded.

What is happening! Why are they running towards the stage?! Those were two of the many questions that swirled through my head as the men appeared out of nowhere. I thought they were there to stop the fight; but to my amazement they threw me off the stage and attacked me like a pack of angry wolves, kicking and barraging me with punches. The blows were coming hard, deadly at least; I felt as though it were my last night. I was in and out of consciousness as people scurried to leave the dance. I was trampled on, and then came the gunshots like pouring rain. It felt like eternity until the sound waned; I was dying. Who would have thought tragedy would have engulfed that beautiful evening?

It started exceptionally exciting. I sipped the champagne as my friends, and I planned our outfit for the dance; we were building the momentum for an awesome time. We finally got to the dance, but at the entrance to the venue, my shoe heel broke- a sign that I should have aborted my plans, but I stilled the voices in my head, knelt, fixed my heel, and made a grand entrance. Celebrity style with all eyes on me.

As I walked into the dance, the air waves reverberated with music from my favorite dancehall sound system, the Military Sound Crew. Immediately the DJ echoed, "Big up Yvonne Gangsta and Shelly Bless." The bottles started popping and the music continued beating, I smelled the strong ganja mixed with the cologne and perfume in the atmosphere. The DJ's welcome communicated a message that attracted the ears of the videographer who immediately started circling the crews and ensuring that those deemed important were kept in the video light. As a result, the crews present started moving towards the middle of the dance floor flashing their expensive name brand clothes and hair styles.

They also began throwing words and talking in the video camera; not everyone liked us, and the feelings were mutual as some of our friends had switched allegiance on us. Amid the outbursts, the DJ started sending shout out to our crew, welcoming us back from Jamaica; we were the hot girls, the talked about crew. I was considered the hypest/hottest.

I felt fired up, so I went on the stage, took the microphone, and began shouting out to The Toppa Top Crew, The Fly Girls and all the rest of the crews which made the promoter of the dance really mad. He did not want me on the stage and began to complain. It was apparent that he did not like me or my friends as he immediately hurled curse words at me, calling me a robber and a thief. I did not understand where he was coming from, we were at a packed dance, and he was trying to embarrass me in front of the crowd. The entire situation became rather awkward, and we got into an altercation on the stage. We were all aggressively grabbing each other, and a fight began. Immediately a group of intoxicated men attacked me. They threw me off the stage and I landed on my back with them on top of my body kicking and punching me. People started running, I fell, and they trampled me on the floor. There on the dancehall floor I begged God for one more chance, to save my life, to allow me to see my children…then the stretcher came.

Chapter 2
Childhood

My mother and aunt were absent from our home, but we never lacked being loved; they migrated to Canada when I was at the tender age of two. The responsibility of raising the children; myself, my newborn brother and our cousins fell on the shoulders of our grandparents until we were all filed for and relocated to Canada. Our grandparents owned the one stop grocery and variety store at the crossroads of the village where we lived.

Mama worked hard at the shop while Daddy worked on his farm. Daddy also worked as a butcher. He was my favourite because he did not beat us. Daddy called me "Pum Pum", I guess because I was a plump, vibrant little brown-skinned girl. I especially loved going to the "Gron" or garden with Daddy to plant seeds, watch them grow and bloom into a fruit. Daddy was a real provider; he always brought home yam and potatoes. He never came home without bringing something for Mama to cook for the family. Being children, we played "Ring around the Rosie," and "There's a Brown Girl in the Ring" with the neighbours. My brother always put me in the ring and that felt great.

Mama was always a hard-working woman, but she was the disciplinarian- she did the beating. I remember not wanting to go to school, but Mama would have none of it. She chased me into the bushes but that day I escaped and hid until school ended. Mama wanted the best for us. Our uniforms had to be neatly ironed and worn. For church we stood out, beautiful frilled dresses and socks for the girls and a suit with bow tie for my brother. Being at church meant sitting quietly listening or deal with Mama's eyes or pinch and if we cried the situation would become worse. Along with her family, Mama was very keen about her business; she kept the customers in check. Subsequently, when one of the citizens decided to steal cigarettes from the shop, Mama chopped him on the hand with a machete.

Our house was attached to the shop, so Mama spent most of her time at the back washing, cooking, and rearing the chickens. When the chickens laid eggs, we took pleasure in gathering them from among the dried cane leaves and bringing them to Mama. Childhood was really exciting.

The Toy

Rainy days were always a treat but not for me. Being influential leaders of the community, my grandparents' shop would be the meeting place, especially on the rainy days. It used to rain a lot and the days would get very dark leaving the patrons with nothing to do but play dominos, chit chat and drink alcohol. Unfortunately, while others were having clean fun, a family friend thought otherwise. He enjoyed calling me to sit in his lap where he would fondle my private parts. I always wondered what Mama would do if she learnt about what he did to me. I wondered if she would have chopped off his hands and finally teach him a lesson for touching and squeezing my private parts. After all, I was only five years old, but I always answered his call because he allowed me to believe he was doing something wonderful. He told me that I was his wife hence his reason for touching me and no one else should be allowed to do the same. Sadly, until I migrated to Canada, rainy days meant I was his little toy.

School is out

The rain stopped, the patrons left and surprisingly Mama told us that we would not attend school the following day- we had to do our medical. The doctor worked in Montego Bay, which meant walking at least a mile for the bus. After the doctor's appointment, Mama went to the market then to visit family members that were living in the town. However, that did not sit well with us as we wanted to return home before nightfall and the bus stopped operating. At nights our village was very dark and scary. To make matters worse, our eldest cousin told us that at nights a creature called the Rolling Calf which had features of a bull with a chain hanging around its neck would capture people. She said the rolling calf was a butcher who transformed into that creature after death. Having listened to her story I wondered if Daddy was going to be a rolling calf when he died.

    We spent all day in Montego Bay. Mama did not understand time because the bus that went back to our village stopped operating after a certain hour. Finally, we took the bus en route home, but it was too late, darkness was already on the land and the closer we got to the village the darker it became. We exited the bus at the nearest bus stop to our village but that still meant walking miles to get home. The journey was rather scary. Mama decided to walk closer to the bamboo trees to avoid any thieves from seeing us and also being seen by approaching vehicles. I was so afraid that I put mama's dress over my head and just followed her steps.

Daddy Spilled the Beans

After that heart wrenching experience, we arrived home; but Daddy was not there. I wanted him to get home before the rolling calf came to capture people that night. I was always worried for Daddy as he loved to walk at nights and tell "Duppy" ghost stories. Suddenly I heard a singing, and I was relieved because I knew Daddy was coming home. He was singing, "My Bonnie rolls over the ocean, my Bonnie rolls over the sea…" that song meant Daddy had done his normal evening's routine; after stopping at his friend's bar, he was now drunk. When Daddy came into the house, we all ran to hug him, but that night was different. Daddy said, "Pum Pum, you are going to live with your mom." "What?" I thought, "What is this man talking about?" Then he continued" Pum Pum is leaving me". "I would never leave Daddy, what is he saying?"

"Was the alcohol talking through him?" "Why did Daddy sound so sad?" Mama interrupted him "Papa, stop telling the children foolishness!" That conversation had me worried; I did not want to leave Mama and Daddy. I did not want to leave my siblings; that was my family.

Mama was the type of person we could not ask questions so that left us to wonder, what was Daddy talking about?... A few weeks later Mama called me into the room and admitted that Daddy was telling the truth. Immediately, I felt the tears running down my eyes, my little world was closing in on me. Mama said that I would be leaving first, then my cousin Alma and Brother Gregory would come after, but I should not tell anyone in the community because people were wicked and they would try to "obeah" which means witchcraft me. Mama took the opportunity to share with us information about Miss Keg's lifestyle; an old woman living in the village. It was rumored that she visited the Obeah man to cast spells on the prosperous people and children in the village. Eventually Miss Keg got really sick and was literally crying and praying that God would take her life, but she could not die. Mama thought she was being punished for all the evil she did to others. On seeing Miss Keg's suffering, I promised Mama that I would remain silent.

Not Again

Our neighbors and family members would visit on weekends. On one particular weekend there was a Nine Night, a kind of celebration for a dead person's relative to show their last respect. Everyone was outside eating and drinking while my cousin and I were inside playing with our dolls and admiring the pretty clothes that our mothers sent us from Canada. While in the room, one of our neighbors, an older lady entered, after which my little cousin ran outside to show off her gifts to our family members, but I stayed inside. After a while, the neighbor told me to lie beside her, and she started squeezing my breasts and touched my private areas. Then, she took my fingers and massaged her vagina. With my inexperience and tiny hands, I failed to please her which caused her to press hard on my hands and to yell at me.

She threatened me not to tell anyone or else I would be punished. I thought what she was doing was okay because someone had done it to me every time it rained. However, when she told me not to tell anyone, with the seriousness in her eyes, I realized that it was something bad.

Departure

In the midst of pain, salvation came knocking. Our church was having a missionary event and Missionaries came to our village. I had never seen white people before, so I stood in awe looking at them. I remember one of the ladies approached me; she had a beautiful smile I could never forget. She told me that Jesus loved me then handed me a small black Bible with John 3:16 highlighted. I never saw that lady again; but I never forgot what she said about Jesus loving me. What the lady said was welcoming but was not sufficient to ease my pain as I was still not prepared to leave my family.

My suitcase was all packed, but my heart was not. Mama and Daddy talked with me the night before I left for Canada.

They said, "Pum Pum, behave yourself when you go to Canada and make us proud of you." At that moment I wished I could run away and hide like I did that day when Mama was chasing me and I hid from her. "Who was going to protect me now?" I thought. My brother would not be there. I remember walking many miles to school with my siblings, and I used to get tired because I was chubby, but my brother would hold my hand and pull me whenever we thought the Black Heart man was coming. The Black Heart Man, a tale that was told to us as children, was the one who would kidnap, kill children, and sell their hearts and lungs. My Brother was our hero and bodyguard. Whenever he heard a vehicle approaching, he would push us into the bushes and cover us with his body. While at school, he would pick mangoes for us and although he was the shortest, he was our strong defense. Now all those precious moments with my cousin and brother would soon be a distant memory.

    The trip to the airport was quiet, a deafening silence. Finally, I arrived at the Norman Manley International Airport. My grandparents brought me to the check in counter and I saw a white lady coming towards me with a big smile. ``Good Morning" she said, she introduced herself to us and then Mama handed me to her. I started bawling. Mama gave me the eye but that could not stop me this time. ``Please Daddy do not let them take me" I cried. I could tell that they too wanted to cry but they held back the tears. At that moment, Mama assured me that the trip was good for me as I needed to see my mother, but we would see each other at summertime. I held the stewardess' hand but kept a firm stare until I could not see my grandparents anymore. The stewardess took me to my seat on the plane; I got a window seat which allowed me to see Mama and Daddy on the airport balcony waving at me.

The flight took off…seat belts please, I awoke from sleeping to the voice of the pilot informing us that we were about to land "Wow! Is this heaven?" I asked myself as I saw the amazing lights from the window. My heart was beating so hard, I had never seen so many lights. Finally, the plane landed, the stewardess and I exited, and she carried me through immigration and then to my mother. My mom seemed very happy to see me and my sisters were also elated. My first night away from my family, everything looked different. My sisters were so excited to see their big sister for the first time. I remember my stepfather laughing and saying, "oh so this is Pum Pum."

As I said everything seemed foreign; In Jamaica we lived in the country/rural area, so we never had a flush toilet, we had oil in our lamps, and we never had a television, as a matter of fact, I had never seen one before. Even the food was different. I felt overwhelmed. I was suddenly in a new place and around strange people. Being my first night in Canada, my mom said I could sleep in the bed with her and my stepfather. Maybe my mom thought that I was scared, and she probably wanted to comfort me. However, my mom did not feel like my mother, after all for the eight years of my life, I did not remember spending any time with her. My grandmother told me a lot about her. On special holidays she would ship a barrel to Jamaica with lots of pretty dresses and dolls for me. Also, church pants, shoes, and toy cars for my brother. However, we always thought that Mama and Daddy were our parents. We knew our mother loved us, but she never expressed it in hugs or kisses. Mama said that she worked really hard to have us live in Canada so she could give us a better life.

Feelings of Discomfort

His laughter at the airport, his demeanor, something, an eerie feeling about my stepfather reminded me of Winston. At bedtime he looked at me and said with a grin, "You're growing into a big woman, and you even have breasts." At that time, the comment seemed innocent to me, that night I slept between both him and my mother.

I could hardly sleep because I missed Daddy's singing, Mama's praying and my brother kicking me out of the bed. The next morning, I awoke to the smell of something frying. I jumped out of my bed and headed straight to the kitchen. I used to love when Mama cooked and called us to the table. I remember my brother trying to steal my dumpling and I would complain to Mama, she would promise my brother the belt if he did not behave himself. My stepfather made sausage and eggs, but he called the sausage hot dogs. I thought in my mind that I am not going to eat any dog. I told my stepfather that I did not want the hot dog; however, he said I had no choice, but to eat. Well, I ate the hot dog and the eggs, but my stomach had other plans. I started vomiting all over the floor, and my stepfather was not pleased about that.

    I wanted to imitate my sisters by calling my stepfather daddy, but every time I tried, it did not sit well with me or him. I never met my real dad. I heard that my father lived in Jamaica, but when I came to Canada; my auntie told me that my dad was in Canada. Will the real dad please show himself? I was completely okay with having my grandfather as daddy. Why did my auntie and stepfather agree that my father lived in Canada? Everyone said a certain man was my father, but that statement made my mother rather upset.

Chapter 3
Adjusting to Canada

I arrived in Canada in the summer. My little sister, Livette, and I went to the park, but things were different, I had to keep a close eye on her. We were at the park, but I really missed home. I missed Mama and Daddy and I really wanted to be with my brother and cousin. We used to play with each other while Mama cooked. We chased lizards and one day the lizard literally turned back and started to chase after me. I started running and I fell between two rocks and bruised my shoulder. The bruise left a mark for life that would always remind me of that day.

School!! What a Dread?

I felt that Canada was in the sky because the plane went up into the air. I also believed that I could dig my way back to Jamaica. Therefore, as I sat in the park, I started digging but all I could see was dirt and rocks, I did not see Mama and Daddy. September came fast and it was time for school. My mom went shopping for us. She bought me runners and jeans with long sleeve sweaters; I did not like the school clothes mother bought for me, maybe because I was used to wearing uniforms. I thought my mother would have bought me nice dress clothes like the ones I wore to church in Jamaica; after all I was living in Canada now, I was a foreigner. My first day at school was awkward. I tried my hardest to fit in and make new friends but quickly realized that it was not as easy as back home. My pretty brown skin was not that pretty to anyone there. John, this white boy started to call me fatso, and everyone began laughing.

Nobody ever called me that name before. Nobody would ever call me names because my brother would have put them in their place. My grandmother told me, "Pum Pum, you are a pretty brown skinned girl." Back in Jamaica everyone loved me. Now I was sitting in a different ring, and everyone was laughing at me. What happened to the Brown Girl in the ring? Now I was just a fat girl in the ring. That did it, I could not bear the name calling, and I got into trouble. The principal called my mom because I punched John in his face, and everyone stopped laughing. Of course, my mother yelled at me and threatened to send me back home to Mama and Daddy. I wanted to go back home, "Maybe I should start punching everyone in their faces, I thought. The difference made my world rather frustrating.

Before I went to bed that night, I pondered, "Why would John call me fat and why were the kids laughing at me?" Maybe it was my clothes. I hated my school clothes. With the anguish of the day, I fell asleep with Mama and Daddy on my mind.

The next morning, I had a plan. I was awake but I stayed in bed pretending that I was asleep because my mother was still at home preparing lunch and getting ready for work. As soon as my mother left with my baby sister, I ran into her room and straight to her closet. I took out a nice top and one of her green high heel shoes. I decided that morning, that was what I was going to wear to school. Nobody was going to laugh at me again or so I thought.

One of my responsibilities was to prepare and take my other little sister to school. She kept drumming in my ears that I could not wear my mother's clothes to school. When I could not get her to stop talking, I told her that if she said anything, I would slap and call the boogeyman on her. I got dressed and we were on our way out the door and headed for school. I felt awkward walking in my mom's heels, but I was determined to wear them.

As soon as we left the apartment building that morning, and started towards the sidewalk, I heard my auntie shouting from the upper balcony, where she lived, at the top of her voice. She yelled at me that I had better get back into the apartment and take my mother's clothes and shoes off. Some of the kids that were there started laughing at me. I did not understand. I thought that I looked really lovely but all I could feel was shame.

    The second day of school started on a bad note and as the hours went by, I realized nobody wanted to be my friend. On my way to lunch, I saw John, the same little boy fighting with Marianne. Marianne was not just one of my classmates but also one of the prettiest girls in the school. She dressed like a tomboy and acted badly but I wanted to be her friend. My opportunity came on that day because John was hitting her real hard until he fractured her hand. I did not like John because he made everyone laugh at me and called me names, I had never heard before. He made everyone hate me. I was so angry that day that I ran towards him and started beating him. I hit him so badly that the principal called my mother again. However, I was not perturbed because I gained a best friend for the rest of my life and all the kids wanted to be my friend.

    Marianne and I did everything together. Every morning we had to bring our younger siblings to school before we went to our class. Marianne had an older sister who was always sad; I always wondered what was wrong with her. She would stare outside her window and watch us play outside. One day Marianne told me that every time her mother went to work; her stepfather would rape her sister, which made me wonder about my stepfather. I was never comfortable being around him, the way he would look at me like an old pervert with a slimy grin.

Adjusting to another environment

Some months went by, and I was slowly adapting to school and to my new family. Everything was looking good. By now, everyone knew that they could only call me fatso behind my back. One afternoon, at lunch time, we were all skipping in the schoolyard and suddenly, I saw floaters moving around aggressively in my right eye; I did not know that it was called floaters at that time. I was so scared I dropped the skipping rope. I told my teacher, and she called my mother who left work early to come to the school. My mother did not handle problems well; she always resorted to cursing and yelling instead of comforting us. I was afraid of what was going on with my eyes, but I was more afraid of my mother yelling at me for something that was not my fault.

My mother took me to many optometrists who only referred me to other eye specialists. The last eye specialist told her I had a bug in the back of my eye. Could that have been the same bug that flew into my eye back home at the water tank? I remembered that day clearly, how much pain I felt and how worried I was, thinking that maybe someone found out that I was going to Canada, and they put a spell on me. But I did not tell anyone, I followed Mama's instruction and kept it a secret.

In the midst of all that was happening to my eyes, I got the news that my parents were moving us to Rexdale. I felt like going into a hole and covering myself with dirt. The thought of leaving my best friend Marianne, and my other friends was not welcoming. I did not want to go to another school. Unfortunately, we moved at the end of the summer that year.

Most of the people in the Rexdale neighborhood were white and they were just staring at us when we were moving in. Mother brought me and my sister to register in our new school, Clearville Secondary. First, it looked as though my sister and I were the only coloured kids.

A new school plus the aggressive floaters in my right eye made me worried. Worst of all, based on my mother's and aunt's conversation someone was working witchcraft on me. "Why would someone want to work witchcraft on me?" I thought. I was only 11 years old. What would I have done for somebody to want to do something bad to me? I left the house and went outside to play with my new white friends. By this time, I was no longer interested in being a brown girl. I wanted to be a white girl with long blonde hair. I dressed white. My white friends wore lumber boots and jackets- they looked like construction workers. I no longer wanted my mom to cornrow my hair, my white friends' hair was left out and I wanted to be like them so when my mother went to work, I would change my hairstyle.

I never heard from my best friend Marianne; Becca had taken her place. I had a new best friend, Becca. Becca was my neighbor, a red-haired white English girl. Her parents would allow me to visit their house and play. I would invite her over to my house and my mom loved her. She loved to eat Hardo Bread. One night at Becca's house, her sister made us play on the Ouija board. After that night, I felt so scared I decided not to play with that board again. It was about the same month one evening that I came home from school, and I sat in the living room with my sister watching Gilligan's Island, when my right eye got extremely blurry. My heart started beating extremely fast as I thought I was going to lose my sight. I knew something was seriously happening.

I ran into the bathroom, and washed my eyes with water, but that did not work, and I had reservations in telling my mother because I was afraid that she was going to be upset with me. That night, I went to my bed with so much fear. The next morning, I woke up with light on one side of the room and darkness on the other. I thought for a second that I was still sleeping so I tried squinting and rubbing my eyes. I tried everything but the room stayed the same, light on one side and darkness on the other. My heart started racing again and of course I was scared, I was totally blind in my right eye. One of the saddest moments in my life was when I had to tell my mother. I thought maybe she could get help for me, or I would keep it a secret. After I told her that I was blind in my right eye, my mother's expression changed. She looked very confused and sad.

The Obeah practitioners

One evening, after I lost sight in my right eye; my mother called me into her room. She told me that she found this man that could help me. I was so excited that I did not ask her any question. It was not important who the man was, I just wanted to see. Mother and I went to Toronto, I entered a dark house to see a short, long haired chubby Indian man. He invited us to sit around a table with candles lit and a bowl with some kind of substance in it. The house had a strong scent of different kinds of oils, frankincense, and myrrh in the atmosphere. I could also hear dogs growling in the back of the house. I looked through the window towards the backyard and I saw Doberman Pinschers and Pit bulls with chains around their necks.

The obeah man started 'reading' my mother and me, telling us things about ourselves. He told my mother that someone was trying to put a spell on her, but instead of it hitting her, it was transferred to me. After he finished 'reading' her, he asked me to step into a room. I was nervous and I did not want to go, but my mother got mad at me. In the room, the

Indian man took some of the hair from my private area and some from my head. When he was through, he rolled some of the hair into minced meat and brought it to the dogs in the backyard. Then, he gave my mother a list of oils that she had to buy and bathe me. He charged my mother a lot of money to see me. After many months of my mother bathing me in all the oils and prayers, nothing changed; I was still blind in my right eye. With no results and the months going by my mother brought me into a dark basement on Kingston Road to see this woman who promised that by December of that year I would see again.

She gave me a bath in pigeon's blood, onions and all different kinds of oils but by then I was not scared anymore because I had seen it all. After the bath, she then instructed my mother not to bathe me for seven days. At school the next day, nobody wanted to sit beside me because I smelled awful. All the blood stains, onions, and grapefruit had dried in my hair. The children called me names and said that I had cooties, but I did not care because I really wanted to see again. That Obeah woman promised my mother that I would see again.

In December, I had to return to the obeah woman, and I was so excited, I believed in what she said. I cannot forget that as my mother entered the house a young lady approached her and pulled her aside. I felt my stomach turning and I knew something was wrong, I wanted to cry. I saw it on my mother's face, something was definitely wrong. Suddenly, my mother turned around, held my hands and we went through the door. "Where was the lady?" I thought. "She promised me." Why was my mother taking me out of the house?" Later, my mother told me that the obeah woman went blind, and that she was not able to help me, my heart was so weak. My face became very hot, and my eyes were flooded with tears; I wanted Mama and Daddy. I could not take the pain anymore; I wanted to go back home.

I was missing a lot of school and I did not care anymore. I was unsure what to do; I felt helpless. I quickly learnt the art of skipping school and going down to the ravine with my white friends to smoke cigarettes. Sometimes I would steal my mother's cigarettes and we would hide and smoke at nights. At other times, we would hang around the neighborhood's garage and play truth dare and double dare. I was now 13 years old, and I secretly started liking guys. However, I kept that information to myself because I was afraid of the rejection. I struggled with being fat, and at school dances no one ever danced with me.

Chapter 4
Prophet Ezekiel

My mother spent most of her time at the church; that was her new pastime. Each afternoon she left work and attended church; she would come home late at nights. Mom always took me with her to the church. I guess she really believed that Prophet Ezekiel would help me see again. One night my mother told me that Prophet Ezekiel was going to give me a spiritual bath which would act as a shield from evil. She also told me that after the bath, I was going to see again.

The Prophetic Bath

It was a late afternoon and mother and I arrived at Prophet Ezekiel's house. The house was in front of the yard and the church was at the back. We walked inside the house to gain access to the back; this was a private session; no one was at the church except prophet Ezekiel and his assistant Mother Gloria. Mother Gloria was skinny, but she appeared very serious. She was dressed in a long red dress, with a Sikh turban on her head. She also had a lot of cords tied around her waist with scissors and pencils hanging from them. Every time I went to church with my mother she would be there, but on that particular day we were few in numbers, so I was more observant. Although she looked serious, she was a very gentle lady.

Prophet Ezekiel told Mother Gloria to prepare a bath. Even though I was used to having these baths by now, a feeling of fear came over me. At that moment my heart started racing. I believe my mom knew something strange was going on with me because she turned around and told me not to be afraid. Then I heard Prophet Ezekiel calling me into the dark bathroom. While in the bathroom all I could hear around me were pigeons cooing. The air in the room was stifling, but it was a scent to which I had grown accustomed. The room was filled with the same kinds of oils, different kinds of herbs and things that were used to make the spiritual baths. Prophet Ezekiel told me to take my clothes off. My mother was in the other room with Mother Gloria, only the Prophet and myself were in that room, so I nervously took my clothes off. I was so cold from standing naked in the dark room I was literally shaking like a leaf.

I saw Prophet Ezekiel taking a pigeon out of the cage; he held the head while I severed it with the knife he gave me. He then squeezed the pigeon's blood into the bath water. I felt like my nerves got shattered; I promised myself that I was going to run away from home and never see my mother again. The Prophet took another pigeon and repeated the same ritual.

While I was being bathed by Prophet Ezekiel, he started telling me how I have a nice sized vagina.

I was wondering, 'why was he talking to me like that? Wasn't he there to help me? Wasn't he a priest? Why is he looking at my vagina? Why was the size of my vagina any of his business?' I just kept quiet until the bath was over. I did not want to say anything because I did not know what would happen to me inside there. My mom was not around, nobody was around; it was just me, Prophet Ezekiel, the pigeons, his knife, and all of those things, so I just kept scared and quiet.

After the bath, he told me to get dressed even with the bloodstains, oily smells, and other herbs all over my body. "This is it," I thought. "No more baths." No more of these things. We went back into the church where my mother and the assistant were waiting. I thought it was time for me to go only to hear the prophet tell his assistant to get the glass of water from off the altar. The altar looked like the round seal that was in the middle of the church; It had lots of fruits, glasses, and candles on it. The glass looked as though it had been there for years. It had a thick green fungus line around the edge, and the water seemed dirty.

He gave me the water, and I was wondering "Why is he giving me this dirty water? I'm not going to drink this." Then he said to me, "Drink the water." I looked at my mom and she was looking at me. She did not say a word, but gave me a stern look, so I drank the water.

Then he administered a milky liquid into my right eye. My stomach felt sick from the dirty water, and my right eye was burning the hell out of me. Mother just sat there without saying anything. I guess my mom did not know what to think or say, she simply wanted my eye to be healed. Little did she know that all those things were hurting me. I was tired of my mother's newfound church and all that was happening there. My eye was not healing. I was tired of those obeah men, or 'witch doctors' as some would call them. It was all fake to me now, all the promises for me to see were all a hoax. Nobody knew what was wrong with my eye. I had gone to so many eye specialists. I had a cataract removed and still, nothing changed.

I was invited to a different church on several occasions, but I kept passing by every time I was going home. One evening I decided to go to the church, Faith Cathedral on Martin Grove, and Albion. It was a fairly big church, and it was so different from the previous one I was attending. No one there was wearing uniforms or turbans on their heads or jumping around and pushing people down. Notably, there was no one beating people for doing sinful acts. I felt a little uneasy because of my dressing, it was different. At my mother's church I had to wear white scarf tied around my head; not many persons covered their heads except for a few people wearing their nice, beautiful fancy church hats. I was sitting in the extreme back of the church when I heard the pastor saying anyone needing prayer should come to the altar. I was 13 years old at that time, and I remember thinking' "as a young girl I needed more prayers than everyone put together in this huge church that I was standing in.' In the midst of it all, I remembered the obeah man, the priest telling my mother that someone had tried to bewitch her, but she had a strong spirit; therefore, the duppy - what others call a ghost - attacked me instead.

I was blind in my right eye because someone wanted to hurt my mother. Unfortunately, all the blood baths I took were not enough to heal me. Hence, the priest told my mom to buy a necklace with a pendant and bring it to him, after he did what he had to do with the necklace; my mother went to pick it up. She placed it around my neck and told me never to remove it; she said that it was called a guardian chain which meant that spirit guides were placed in the pendant and wherever I went, the spirits went with me. She also told me that the priest warned that if the pendant fell off my neck, an evil spirit would attack me.

One day I was in my yard playing in the rain with my best friend Becca and the guardian chain fell off my neck. Immediately I got scared and ran so hard to my house. While I was running, I felt as if I were being chased by demons. The fear that I felt was unexplainable, I thought I was being attacked from every angle. I did not know what to do. When I told my mother she got extremely angry with me. She kept saying, "I warned you about keeping that necklace on." "Maybe I was just going to die," I thought. "Maybe this was the last of me. I was just tired of everything. Every day it was something new, I could not take it anymore, I was simply ready to die."

The Change Came

Well, there I was standing at the altar in the church in front of the pastor. How did I get to the front of the altar? I was not sure, but I was there. I was thinking maybe the pastor could pray for my eye. The pastor prayed for me and asked me if I wanted to accept Jesus into my heart. He also prophesied and told me that my mother was in a bad place, and that one day, I would help her out of it. He said she was in a church where they practiced witchcraft; he continued to say that it was demonic. The pastor prayed for me, and I accepted Jesus in my heart. That night I went home, and I told my mother that I was going to get baptized. She was happy for me, but nobody showed up at my baptism. I did not care because I felt like a new person. I loved going to my new church. I was a new person although I was still blind in my right eye.

The Unexpected Came

One day when I came home from school and everyone, including my aunt and my cousins were all at my house, based on the look on their faces, I could tell something was terribly wrong. My auntie turned towards me and said "Pum Pum, Daddy died." She meant my grandfather back home. My heart started to race, and I felt warm tears running down my face. As a child growing up, I never saw anyone else as my dad, except my grandfather. He was who I knew as my daddy. He was the only father I knew. Nobody loved me like daddy did.; now he is gone. Mother was planning on sending me to visit in the summer holiday. Our tickets were already bought, and everyone's suitcases were packed; I felt sad, but was happy that I would see my brother.

We travelled and we arrived in the village, it was dark, but the yard was still filled with family and friends. As soon as I entered the yard, I ran to find my brother. I was so happy to see him. Then I ran to hug Mama. I did not want to see my uncle; I was told by my mother that my uncle Shane chopped my grandfather with a machete and that is why he died. My uncle was my grandmother's last child. I felt really angry yet elated. I cried because Daddy was gone, but I was also happy to be home. He, my uncle, was very spoiled. Whenever he did not get his way, he tried to beat us up and attack my parents/grandparents. Whenever my uncle went on his attacks, stoning the house with huge rocks and breaking the windows, Mama would cry profusely and hold her breast towards the sun and ask God to take him. I seriously thought that he would have killed me; he did not like me much because I was my grandfather's favourite.

After arriving, we sat with my aunties from the United States of America, uncles and extended family on the verandah talking about Daddy, then I looked up and I saw this guy coming towards the house. I knew the face, but at first, I did not remember the name. Oh! It was Courtney, one of my school mates. We used to walk to school together and play as well. Courtney was afraid of Mama, so he wanted me to meet him outside the yard. When I met with him, he told me how much he missed me when I left; he held my hands and immediately I felt Goosebumps all over my body. No boy ever told me that they liked me or even took hold of my hands. Then the unexpected happened; he told me that I was his girlfriend. I felt good on the inside. I wanted to play truth or dare and double dare all over again because I knew that this time, I would get the kiss that I had been longing for. Back in Canada I was in love with this white boy Brian and whenever we played truth or dare and double dare, I always wanted him to land on kiss, but it never happened. Now I was standing in front of my first kiss, but I had to go inside because I heard my mom calling me. I explained to Courtney that I would see him a few days later at the Nine Night.

A 'Nine Night' is something like a party or a celebration that the family would have to show the last respect for the dead. I was so anxious for that night to come; I wanted to see Courtney again. After the special moment with Courtney, I finally got a chance to talk to Mama. She cried and told me how much she missed Daddy. Then, she told me to tell my mother to apply for my brother, because soon my cousin would migrate to Canada, and she did not want him to be left in Jamaica on his own. I told her that I would try my best.

The Nine Night finally came, and everyone started coming into the yard. The music was playing, people were drinking, gathering, and playing dominoes and other games. I did not see Courtney and I started to feel disappointed; I thought he was going to let me down. I thought that he was not going to come and that it was all a joke. "Maybe he did not like me," I thought. Then I looked up and there he was looking straight at me; he used his finger to call me over to him. I snuck out of the big yard. I thought no one saw me but I was wrong. There was my brother right behind me trying to protect me as usual. I told him that Courtney and I were just going for a walk and that we would be back soon. I also told him not to tell anyone and he agreed.

Courtney held my hands again, but this time he drew my body closer to his. We were so close that I could feel his heart beating and the hot air coming from his breath. I wanted him to kiss me so badly, but I did not want him to know so I acted shy. Then I felt his lips pressing against mine, and suddenly I was in another world. I did not want to let go, I wanted to be in his arms for the rest of my life. I had no desire to return to Canada; nobody wanted me there. Unfortunately, the fairy tale was interrupted by my brother's voice. I quickly pulled away from Courtney and ran back to the yard. My brother said that my mother was searching for me. Of course, my first kiss had to be broken up by my mother who wanted to show somebody how I had grown.

The Nine Night was soon over, and the yard was empty. We all went into the house and talked until we fell asleep. I dreamt about Courtney all night; I wanted him to be my boyfriend.

I will never know if anyone saw Courtney and me talking that night, but for the rest of the vacation, all eyes were on us. Courtney could only come to the fence and after a while I never saw him again. The day of the funeral came, and the entire village was there. It was like a celebrity funeral; people from different parishes were at Daddy's funeral. I cried so hard, I thought my heart was going to burst, and then it was over. The place became so quiet, the yard was empty and the whole village was hushed. It was all over and now it was time for us to start packing our suitcases.

That night while packing, I got a chance to ask my mother about applying for my brother to live with us in Canada. I remember crying to my mother about my brother and telling her that it would be bad for him to stay in Jamaica with family members; she promised that she would work on it when she returned to Canada. My brother coming to Canada would be one of my dreams come true.

Newness

I was 13 years old, and my menstruation/period started; I did not like the idea. I learned about it at school. Mother never really talked to me a lot about sex, or having my period, so I did not know how to tell her. It was my secret, and I did not want anyone to know. I finally gathered up the courage to tell her. Why did my mother tell my stepfather? I did not want him to know. I was never comfortable talking to him about anything or to even be alone in the house with him. The relationship with my stepfather was not good and it was deteriorating. He treated my stepsister's way better than he ever treated me. Thankfully, my auntie moved closer to where we were living in Rexdale. It was easy for me to walk from our house to her apartment building on Kipling Avenue. I used to visit my auntie on the weekend in order to spend time with my cousin, Alma. My brother had not yet migrated to Canada, so we only had each other. We both came to Canada before my brother did. With the passing of time, I no longer wanted to live with my mother. Before my auntie migrated to Canada, she helped Mama to care for us; we missed her when she left to live in Canada. I told my mother that I wanted to stay with my auntie Ina and my cousin Alma. My aunt was married to Uncle Irvine who was always at work at nights. My auntie's house felt like home, like family. Mama migrated and lived with auntie Ina; my brother was the only one left to migrate.

Chapter 5
New Friends

My cousin and I used to visit the park where we met Pat and Idene; they became our best friends. Pat and Idene lived with their mother and their little brother, but their mother worked at nights as well. They were always stuck taking care of their brother. As a result, we always had to take him with us everywhere we went, except on weekends when his dad was home. Additionally, we met Garcia, an older girl living in a group home; she became one of our best friends as well. Garcia's mother had died, and she was living with her father. Unfortunately, her father would have his friends visit the house where they would play dominos, drink, and often rape her. Garcia said that she would always run away from her home, but her father would find and beat her really badly. Thankfully, someone called the Children's Aid Society, and she was placed in a group home. At nights, we would go by the group home, and she would climb out the window. We started going to parties in the area.

Garcia taught us to steal clothes from the shopping malls and the laundromat. When we were caught stealing clothes, the police placed us on curfews because we were too young to go to jail. Whenever the police went to my apartment my grandmother who relocated to Canada shortly after Daddy died, was the one to answer the doorbell and collect the curfew papers. I told my grandmother not to tell my aunt because I would have to return to my mother's house. My grandmother knew that my stepfather treated me badly so she would not tell auntie what the police said.

As soon as my grandmother fell asleep, we would all gather to attend the parties happening inside the apartment building. Inside the parties would be really dark. There would be loud music, people smoking weed and women leaning against the wall with men hard pressed on their bodies. I remember that the only time a boy ever pressed so hard on me was when I got my first and only kiss from Courtney. Now I was ready to be kissed again.

The Dance Floor

By now we were all on the wall dubbing with someone, which was the popular dance at the time. A female would have her legs parted and backed against the wall. The man would go between her legs, and they both would start moving their bodies against each other. One particular night, I was dancing my life away when a Rasta guy came in with his friends. I could not dance anymore; I just stared at the guy. I loved the way he walked. He had really long dreads, and a straight nose. He was so handsome. He did not even notice me, but I guess it was too dark. However, I could see him clearly.

He walked over to the DJ booth, took the microphone, and started to DJ. An air of jubilation broke out as the people shouted for him to DJ more. On my way home, I could not stop thinking about the guy. I liked everything about him. "I was in love," I thought. I wanted to be everything that he was. I asked Garcia if she knew who he was and she told me that he would frequent Jamestown, and Orpington-volatile areas. She also told us a lot of stories about things that happened to her in the town. I went to my bed with him all over my heart. I never felt this way about anyone in my life.

One morning while on the balcony I saw Backy, the Rasta guy from the dance floor. By now, I knew his name, and I also heard that he had a baby mother, but he was not with her. I was so in love I started twisting my hair because I wanted to have dreadlocks like he did. I wanted to dress like him. I began wearing long skirts with red, green, and gold belt; those are the colours that the Rastas wear. I would wear those colors on my hat and my belt.

One day I saw him from my balcony, walking towards my building. I wanted to see him closer, so I called my cousin, and we got the rest of the girls. We went to the first floor of their apartment building and there he was playing dominoes with his friends. He was staring at me and right then and there, I knew that Garcia told him that I liked him. She could never keep a secret. He walked over to me and asked me for my number. Oh, I felt the blood flushing through my face. Was this really happening? Maybe it was a good thing that Garcia told him…how else would he have known?

We exchanged numbers. However, I hated calling his home because he was never there, and his mother was extremely mean. She was always asking, "Why are you young girls calling here for my son? Leave my son alone!" Garcia told us that the town was really bad, but I did not care because I wanted to see Backy, so we started going to more parties. One night we went to a basement party, it was packed but my crew and I pushed through the crowd because I wanted Backy to see that I was there. When I heard him Deejaying over the microphone, I was overcome by a happy feeling. So many guys were pulling at us to dance, but I did not want to dance with them. When Backy finished Deejaying, he walked over to me.

No questions asked, he knew that I wanted him to dance with me. He pushed me against the wall, and we began dancing. It was dark and hot. I could feel us sweating on each other. Then suddenly, I felt my second kiss. He wanted me to leave the party with him. I was afraid to go because I knew what was coming next. I was afraid. I was a virgin. For all the stories I heard about losing one's virginity, fear shackled me. When I told him no, he became angry and walked away from me. Thereafter he passed by numerous times at the party but pretended as though I was not there. Following that night, he never called my phone anymore.

The Unthinkable Happened

One afternoon we all decided to go over to the town, the volatile area. All the guys were hanging out at the entrance of the town, I never liked passing by because of them. They were always shouting things like, "Hey sexy!" "Come here!" I thought that they would laugh at me or say something. As a result, I started talking to my friend. I liked to take it slowly because I saw all the guys standing in the town talking, so I pretended that I was talking to Garcia, but she started walking ahead of us. Suddenly one of the guys grabbed Garcia and threw her behind the garbage bin in the town. All the guys started taking turns going behind the bin where Garcia was. We knew that they were raping her, so we started running down the hill across the field. At one point, I thought that we were being chased.

We were so afraid that we forgot about what was happening to Garcia until we arrived home. We finally got a hold of Garcia, "What happened?" we asked her; but she started to curse us. She blamed us for what happened to her. She said that they "battery" her. The term battery was used when a woman got raped by more than one man. Maybe she would have felt better if we all got raped because she was more upset about us running away than getting raped. Later, I realized that she was raped so many times that she became immune to it.

From that day, we decided that the town was off limits; the closest we would go was Rexdale mall to steal clothes with Garcia. We started hanging out around our building. A few weeks had passed, and I had not seen or heard from Backy. The summer was almost over, and my mother wanted me to return home to start my new school, however I was not really ready to leave my cousin, and my friends.

A New Guy

Shortly before I returned to my house, I met Eric at a party. He lived in our building, so we got to see each other all the time. One day, he invited me downstairs to his apartment; his mother was not home. Although Eric was hanging with his brother and the popular guys in the community, he did not act like them; he was a dark skinned, slim, quiet, kind of guy. He always protected me. He was so in love with me, just the way he treated me I knew it. However, for some reason I was never attracted to the good guys. Once, he invited me into his mother's apartment. When we got inside, he wanted me to go into his room; I told him that I was not ready to sleep with anyone. He said that he would not hurt me. I sat on his bed, and he started kissing me, he was so gentle, I felt the love from him until he started to pull my brassiere. I was not having it; I tried pushing him off me but that was not enough. I liked Eric, but my heart was somewhere else. I wished that it was Backy lying on top of me.

Backy was a thug; the way he walked, how he dressed, and his long dreadlocks, that was where my heart resided. Eric started pressing hard on top of me, and I knew he wanted to have sex badly. He kept saying, "Yvonne, I promise I won't hurt you." I finally squeezed my body out from under his, and I ran out of the house. I took the stairs up to my apartment. I ran so hard mama knew something had happened. When mama asked, I lied and said I was running up the stairs to get some exercise, Mama was not convinced.

Since mama migrated to Canada, she did not act the same. Back home, she was always working, always actively taking care of the shop and the chickens, now in Canada she was just stuck in the apartment with nothing to do. If I were in Jamaica with Mama, she would have flogged us for coming into the house late at night. After speaking with Mama, I went into the room I shared with my cousin. She was not at home, so I simply laid on the bed with a sense of relief that I arrived home and I was still a virgin.

"Pum Pum! Pum Pum, someone is on the phone for you!" "Who is it, Mama?" I asked. "Just come to the phone," she commanded. Mama did not like to ask who was calling. My auntie and I tried to tell her on numerous occasions that she needed to ask who was calling and for them to leave a message, mama was not used to that because we did not have any phones in Jamaica. It was Eric that called me. He wanted to know if I was okay, and he apologized for coming on to me so strong. He wanted to know if I was still going to hang out with him. I told him yes, but I really was not sure if I wanted to see him again or even be with him. It was Thursday and the weekend was coming up, that was probably the last weekend staying with my cousin. Eventually Eric became the kind of guy that I would always run to when I felt that I needed that extra attention. Even when I moved away to Scarborough Eric still came to see me, but that visit would be the last.

It Happened

As I laid on my bed, I started daydreaming about being with the Rasta man. I wondered if it would ever happen. "Would I ever be his girlfriend?" I thought. Garcia called and wanted us to meet at the mall. We all went into a boutique where they had a lot of fancy name brand outfits. I told Garcia the one I wanted, and she took it off the rack and put it into her shopping bag that she was carrying. She was a pro at stealing. I was still nervous, but later I became a professional. My cousin, Alma, never stole. She was always afraid, so we had to get what she wanted. Pat and Idene were not afraid either; they both got their outfits for the weekend. The party was at Orpington, a nearby town. We all felt a little safer going to Orpington, because my cousin's boyfriend lived there, and he was popular. He really liked my cousin, and he would have done anything for her, which included protecting us from the thugs. It was Saturday evening, and we all knew exactly what we were going to wear to the party, but we had to wait for my aunt and uncle to leave the house.

Waiting in the apartment with my aunt and uncle was the most nerve wracking, although we knew the time they would leave for work, it seemed like forever. We did our best to keep our composure and keep off any suspicion. Mama knew that we were planning to take off, but she pretended otherwise. Finally, my aunt and uncle left the house, and we left shortly after. We all met downstairs by Pat and Idene's house where we got dressed; we were looking so cool. My cousin was the most beautiful; I always admired her mode of dress and confidence. All the guys would try to get her attention when she refused, they turned to us.

We were now ready to go to the party. We started walking from Kipling to Orpington, a forty-five minutes' walk. While we were walking and talking, I started thinking about Backy. I knew that he was going to be there Deejaying. When we finally arrived in Orpington many people were lined up outside wanting to go into the basement party. Suddenly I heard a lady shouting at us, "where are these little girls going". She continued. "Go home to your yard!!" I wondered "to whom was she referring?! We did not even know her. I wish she would mind her own business." Garcia was always the one to speak out and she told the lady just that. The woman threatened to slap Garcia in her face. We were now at the entrance to the party and a guy appeared from nowhere trying to hit on me; he was so not my type. I did not want to talk with him, he kept calling me browning and telling me how much he liked me in front of everyone that was in the lineup. It was such an embarrassing moment.

I turned around and told him bluntly what he should do to his mother; that was a huge mistake. You never tell a Jamaican man to find pleasure with his mother. I felt a punch that landed me on my back, luckily my cousin's boyfriend and some other guys were there, or he would have beaten me to a frazzle. We left the party to hang out in the parking lot. My face was a little swollen, but we did not want to go home. After a while, my cousin's boyfriend said that the guy that punched me went home. Apparently, he was drunk, so we all went into the party.

As soon as I reached inside the basement, I heard him. I heard Backy. I heard my man; he was deejaying via the microphone. I thought that he would not talk to me because he was probably still mad. I wanted him to see me, so I pushed close to the sound system by the DJ booth. Our eyes connected. He walked over to me, took my hands, and brought me into the corner where we started to dance. I just wanted him to kiss me and that was exactly what he did. I just wanted to give him all of me; whatever he wanted I was ready. The kiss was getting harder, and he wanted us to leave. He left the dance and told me to meet him in the parking lot. I told my cousin and my friends that I was leaving and that I would meet them back at the building.

I was nervous, but I made up my mind. He was the man that was going to take my virginity; the man that I dreamt about every day. Now, I was right there with him. He brought me over to his friend's house who told him that we could go into the room upstairs because nobody was home. In the room, he started kissing me again and I was kissing him back. He started to take my clothes off, and I told him no; I felt embarrassed and scared. I did not want him to see me naked. He told me that I should take my panties off. I took them off and lay down on the bed. He came on top of me, and he took it. He took my virginity. It was so painful I felt the blood soaking the bed. When he was through, he told me to go into the bathroom and clean up myself. After I came back into the room, he said that he had to leave. I did not want him to go; that was my special moment. How could he leave me? I thought he was going to spend the night with me.

I figured that I was now his girl but suddenly everything seemed like a joke to me. He called his friend into the room and told him that he was leaving, he was laughing. He was acting so immature.

Why was he doing this to me? He started telling me that I could spend the night with his friend. His friend said "No, boss. She can't be here. My mother will be coming home from work soon." "Backy," I said, "There isn't any bus running at this time, it's after 2 am." He kept walking towards the door to leave. I started yelling at him and cursing him. I wanted to fight him. He got mad and he took my underwear, ran outside, and threw it into the tree. He left me standing in the middle of Orpington with no underwear on. It was freezing that night. I felt the breeze going up under my legs. My whole body felt so cold, but my heart felt like frozen ice cracking and falling apart. I did not have anywhere to go because it was unsafe for a young girl to walk around in that kind of neighborhood, the only alternative for me was to ask Backy's friend if I could sleep until the morning. He told me under one circumstance; he wanted me to sleep with him. I bluntly told him that I could not; there was nothing left in me. Please, I begged him just to let me sleep until early in the morning. He agreed and I left early in the morning to walk to Kipling by myself without panty, a broken heart, and a swollen face. My walk back home was silent but the thoughts that ran through my mind were unbearable. The tears that flowed from my heart were cold.

Chapter 6
The Runaway

I moved back home to my mom and stepfather, but they relocated again, and we were now living closer to my aunt, which meant I was closer to my cousin and friends. However, it was hard to sneak out of my mother's house to go partying. I was missing out on a lot. I decided that I was going to run away from home to live with my friends. I went to live in the town with my friend's mom.

The Reunion

One day I was walking in the town when I saw this girl with long dreadlocks. She was wearing a pleated skirt, diamond socks with Clarks boots. From a distance she was unrecognizable but as I got closer, I realized that it was my best friend, Marianne; I had not seen her since I moved away from Grand Ravine located in Jane and Finch. We had lost each other's phone numbers; I thought I would never see her again.

Now she had a little boy in a stroller. She told me that he was her baby and that her baby father lived in the town. We caught up on everything. We exchanged new phone numbers and since that day, we have never separated again. Marianne's baby father, Glider, who I had met some time before, was one of the gang leaders in the town. He was medium-height, very handsome with a special walk but he was a boasty (proud) person. Being one of the bad guys in the town, we were afraid of him because he did not take no for an answer. Marianne told me that she was afraid of him too. She said that once he shot her in her foot. Time went by quickly and it was now rather late so Marianne and I left each other's company.

One particular night we followed Garcia into Glider's house where he and his friends were playing dominoes in the basement. The basement was smokey and marijuana literally perfumed the atmosphere. I did not feel comfortable going there so I turned to leave, but there was Glider. He grabbed me and asked, "Where do you think you're going?" I wanted to scream, but no one would have heard me even if I did. He told me to follow him to his room, but I decided that it was not going to happen that night. Even though he called me every name in the book, I did not care; my refusal got me kicked out of his house without my friends. It was a winter night, and the town was very dark, so I went to my friend Cobra's house. His grandmother was there so I had to sleep in the basement until early morning. I already knew what happened to my friends, so I decided not to ask.

Life in the town was scary until you got used to it. The police were always coming into the town, kicking down drug dealers' doors and harassing the men. The men were always robbing each other. People were always fighting - women fighting each other because their baby fathers cheated on them. There were only a few people that just wanted to mind their own business and stayed inside their homes.

Against My Will

Although being at my friend's house made it easier to attend parties I really did not like being there. Her mother would give me a list of groceries for me to steal from the supermarket; I did not know how to tell her no, so I would go whenever she sent me. I was stealing on a regular basis for her even though I was still in secondary school. I would leave my friend's house to go to school but dreaded coming back home. Westway Secondary was more like a trade school. It was a great school, but my mind was not really focused on education.

One day at lunch time, I was hanging around the hallways looking at the graduates' pictures on the wall. There was a yearbook from the previous year that was on the side of the bench, I opened it and started leafing through. Surprisingly, there in the book was a photograph of Backy; class of 1980. I did not know his real name until that day, and I had never seen him at that school before; well, I was a fairly new student. After that night in Orpington, I did not care to see him anyway. Well shortly after seeing the picture guess who I saw in the hallway walking towards me. I thought it was a ghost. He was smiling at me as though he forgot what he did to me. "What are you doing here?" he asked. I thought to myself, 'Obviously, I'm going to school here.' He continued, "How come you don't call me?" "Well, how come you don't call me?" I asked. I did not know why I was even talking to him, but for some reason, it felt good to see him. It was like I missed him, and I did not know it until I saw him.

After that conversation with Backy, I never tried to get intimate with him again. I still had feelings for him, but I managed to control them; sometimes I would see him in the town, but I ignored him. He knew that I really liked him but after what he did to me, I could never forget. I wonder if he understood just how much he hurt me, but I could never find it in my heart to hate him. He was my first love, and nothing could ever change that. **After leaving school**, Backy would always resurface **but a reigniting of the relationship** was never in the picture. I **simply** helped out a few times by giving **him** a room to stay. He was addicted to crack cocaine and needed my help. I tried to help him as much as I could, but he was not improving and I had to kick him out of my house. I never wished bad for him but every time I looked at him, I remembered what he did to me, and I also wondered, "what if he had given me that chance to be his girl?" Probably I would have had his children and being the woman that I became maybe just maybe he would not be in the position that he was in.

New Kid on the Block

Heineken was the name on everyone's lips; he was the new kid on the block, but he did not play around, he was said to be a bad man. One morning I was walking through the town to get on the bus for school and I heard someone calling, "Hey, pretty girl!" I turned around and I saw this tall, fair-skinned, good-looking guy calling me. I held my head straight because after being around the town long enough, I knew what comes with a guy calling you like that, so I kept walking. I walked close to the sidewalk just in case he tried grabbing me I would be able to run. I did not look back; I kept walking until I arrived at the bus stop. It took a while before the bus came, and I finally got on the bus.

It was weird. I settled in the bus and believe it or not I started thinking about the guy that was calling me a few minutes earlier and what it would be like to know him more, especially with that gangster look. Sometime later I learnt that he was Heineken. He also became my dance partner at a party. After dancing, we exchanged phone numbers, and he asked me if I was not going home. I was not ready, but he was not someone that I wanted to argue with hence, I left, and he walked me to the unit that I was staying. After that night we talked at nights via the phone. He told me that he really liked me and wanted me to be his girl. I really wanted to be with him, with someone that would protect me from the rest of the goons.

He had a reputation, and I was so cool with that. I wanted everyone to know that I was with a gangster. **Whenever I visited** my aunt, I would let my grandmother say hi to him on the phone. She liked him; she said he was very respectful. Heineken was more on the private side; **he** did not like to tell people his business. He only told me his first name; everything was a secret. He did not like me hanging out with my friends; I guess he heard about us too. He wanted me to be like a good girl, but I was not having it. I would skip school and hang out with him. He told me to go home to my parents and **stopped** hanging out on the street. I knew that he really liked me.

What Heineken said and the negative attitude from my friend's mom allowed me to see that it was time for me to leave the town; I did not want to steal groceries for her anymore and that made her angry. **I knew I had to go home** but my stepfather made me so uncomfortable there. He always complained to my mom about me going out with my friends **and** I especially did not like the way he l**ooked** at me.

The New Ladies

I told my friends how I felt about my stepfather and **the fact** that I did not want to be at the apartment with just him and my siblings. My mom was always at church, and I decided that I was not going to be his sex toy while she was away. I did not return to my mom, I decided that I was going to move to Tanridge with Idene, Pat and their mom; she was really nice too. She worked at night and slept during the day; that was okay for us because we could go partying at night. I did not hear a lot more from Heineken. I knew that he liked me but he was unable to control my lifestyle so that kept us from being with each other. However, he would still visit me every now and then. He was not like what everyone said about him, at least I did not see it.

During that time a lot happened; my cousin Alma moved to Scarborough, and we hardly spoke to each other. I was still going to school but not as much as my friends and I would skip school to hang out with the boys at the malls; we usually got into a lot of trouble. We met Marjorie, a light skinned lady with bold eyes; she was Idene's neighbor.

    We began spending a lot of time at Marjorie's house; she was older and filled the role as our big sister. A lot of guys would be at her house drinking and chatting. One day a group of ladies visited her house; they were wearing a lot of jewelry and dressed in expensive clothes. I wanted to know who those ladies were. I later found out that they were a part of two separate crews: the Bore Nose Posse, and the Bucca's Crew. All attention was on them when they walked into any party. I started idolizing them and wishing I could be a part of their crews. One day I met Christine Buccas; she lived in Tanbridge, but not in the building, she lived in the townhouses. I used to love visiting her house. She was a Crutcher; a professional booster (thief).

My crew and I used to steal, but we were petty thieves compared to Christine. Christine was older than us; she lived with her two sons and husband who was hardly ever home. I knew this because I started doing a lot of babysitting for her. Her house was the most beautiful; she had nice furniture with various kinds of decorations. Her bedroom was extremely beautiful, and there were so many brand-new clothes and shoes. Christine made a profession from stealing and selling the stolen goods; I wanted to be just like her. She was popular, a fashionista, chubby like me and she had confidence. She did not let her weight get in her way. She was my role model, and I was determined to follow in her footsteps. Christine taught me how to be a professional booster.

The summer was up, and I was not comfortable being at Pat and Idene's anymore, their mother was not as nice to me, maybe I outstayed my welcome. I spent half of the winter and most of the summer in Tanridge then I decided to return to my mother who was now living in Scarborough.

The Sneaky Stepfathers

My mother was in her church as usual, so I was home with my stepfather, grandmother, and siblings. We were living in a beautiful house, and I had my own room, which was good for me because I liked my personal space and I hated when anyone touched my things. Mama slept in my room sometimes which would remind me of life in Jamaica. Mama loved to watch Evangelist Jim Baker, and his wife, Tommy Baker on the Praise the Lord Club (PTL Club). Mama loved the Lord, and she always prayed with us.

It was the end of the summer, and I got enrolled in Timothy Eaton Secondary School. My first year at Eaton was great! I enrolled in drama class and played the role of a Mexican maid; that made me super popular. Everyone, even my teacher, encouraged me to go to drama school. I also met Jody who became one of my best friends. She had recently migrated to Canada; she lived with her mom, stepfather, and her siblings. After a while, we started skipping school and began hanging out at other schools and people's houses. I still dreaded going home after school knowing that my stepfather was there. One particular evening I went home, and my mother was not there. My grandma was always in a room watching TV with my little sister and brother, who migrated from Jamaica. I changed my school clothes and went to watch Gilligan's Island with my brother. I was just about to get comfortable when I heard my stepfather calling me. I walked up the stairs, my heart thumping. He was in the bathroom taking a shower. I could hear the sound of the water running but he was still calling me. "Can you pass me the soap?" he yelled. "There isn't any in the bathroom." I ran to the closet to get the soap. I opened the bathroom door, quickly put it beside the shower, ran out the bathroom and closed the door. Then he called me again, this time he asked me to hand him the soap. I wondered "Why does he want me to hand him the soap?" I stretched my hand to give him the soap, but he grabbed my hands and tried to pull me into the shower.

My hands slipped out of his wet hands, and I ran. I was getting so tired of my stepfather's passes that he constantly made at me. I was worried. If this man raped me, how could I live with myself? What if he got me pregnant? What would happen to me? My new best friend Jody told me that she too wanted to run away from her home. Her stepfather was doing the same thing, and her mother did not believe her. The day came and Jody could not take it anymore. Her stepfather tried to rape her, and she stabbed him with a knife; the wound left him paralyzed. My mom called my attention to the fact that Jody made the news, but she was unaware that after the incident, a scared Jody ran away from home and was hiding in our basement. She was later charged but was soon released because he was trying to sexually assault her.

At that moment I had to be dealing with the same issue. During that time period, it seemed as though all my friends were having issues with their stepfathers. Most weekends I would spend time at my auntie's house with my cousin Alma. My brother knew what my stepfather was trying to do to me but he never said anything; it was not the same as Jamaica, he no longer protected me. I figure everyone was in their own little world or foreign had changed them. Mama changed too but she still tried to protect us. Mama knew what was going on with my stepfather. I remember one night my mother was at church, and our neighbor invited the entire family, my brother, uncle, and stepfather to a basement party. I went because I loved music and I loved to dance. We got to the basement and no sooner than I entered there was my stepfather pulling at me to dance with him. I wondered, "Was this man going crazy?" All our neighbors and friends were at this party.

I felt like my cup had run over; enough was enough. I ran from the basement party to our house. I ran upstairs to my room, "Mama," I said, "I'm tired, and I'm angry." I told mama what my stepfather had been doing. Previously, I wrote a letter that I hid under my mattress. I took it out and gave it to Mama. I noted all the times he made passes at me, and I kept quiet about it, all the times he tried to touch me, and said sexual things to me. That night I felt awkward being in that house. Mama said, "Pum Pum, after all these years that I took care of you, this is not what I sent you to Canada for." Mama told my mother. It was like the old mama reappeared; the no nonsense Mama, the Mama that fought back. She started wearing pants inside the house with a string running through the loops. When my mother asked her why she was wearing her pants in that manner she replied, "there's a rapist in the house; one that wants to rape Pum Pum." my granddaughter.

Chapter 7
Death Threats

Mother was frustrated; she did not know what to do. In my heart I wished that she would take my siblings, grandmother, myself and move out of my stepfather's life. The next evening when I came home from school, my mother came into my room to talk to me. She said that she would be sending me to live with my auntie while she searched for a place for us to move away from my stepfather. I was really going to miss Mama more than anyone else, but I was also excited to go and spend time with my cousin.

I really enjoyed staying at my auntie's but shortly after I got there, she told me that my mother wanted me to return home. I was disappointed. I called mom to enquire why we were not getting a place of our own and she said places were really hard to find. She also confessed that she spoke to my stepfather, and he assured her that he would not bother me anymore. When I returned home, I was so happy to be with my Mama. We spent some time praying together before bed, and I went to church with her. Mama's church was quiet, not much clapping but I loved the serenity when I went to church with her.

At home, my stepfather's silence made me so uncomfortable. He hardly talked to me and sometimes I would see him showing me a bad face. One day I was in my room, and I heard a bang on my room window. As I went towards my window, I saw my stepfather standing at the front looking up at me. As soon as he saw that he got my attention, he raised his hand towards his neck and swiped his finger across his throat, a sign that he wanted to cut my throat. I did not say anything to anyone about his threats on my life because I just did not want any more problems. I saw how frustrated my mom was before and I did not want to say anything else to her again. During that period living at home became extremely difficult for me.

Therefore, I decided to go back to the west end on weekends to visit my friends. I just wanted to be away from my stepfather. My mother continued going to church, and nothing changed except that my stepfather hated me, and I was tired. I tried my very best to stay away from the house.

The Next Level

One midnight, Pat, Idene and I were getting ready to go to a big dance on Jane and Finch at Palisade Community Center; that was a big move considering we only went to basement parties or other types in people's apartments. All the famous dancehall people and the ghetto superstars were there while my little crew and I were like invisible people in that big hall. We were not popular just wannabes. We were hurrying, because unlike everyone else who drove their cars to parties, we would take the bus then a taxi home. When we arrived at the party, I saw my cousin Patty. Well, she was not really my cousin, but her mom was my mother's best friend and she used to babysit my siblings and me when we were younger.

I think she was a part of the Bucca's Crew or the Bore Nose Posse as they called themselves. The place was packed like sardine, but it was obvious that Patty was the best dressed lady there; I could not tell her though as I was hiding. I feared maybe Patty would tell me to go home or probably tell my mother, therefore my crew and I stayed in the corner of the room watching the Bucca's Crew and the Bore Nose Posse dancing in the middle, all eyes were on them. Then I saw all the gangsters rolled in and I wished I was in the middle with them; they were the most talked about posse in the city. Christine Bucca was also in the middle dancing while the DeeJay kept saluting her.

In the midst of my thoughts, I felt someone touching me from behind. I turned around, and there was a guy. He said, "Baby, can I dance with you?" I could not resist because I loved Rubba Dubbing. We started winning on each other and he told me he was from Jane and Finch. Then the disappointment came; again,

I felt a pat on my back and yes it was my cousin Patty. I stopped dancing. "Go home little girl. What are you doing at an adult party?" She spoke so loudly that people were looking at me; I felt so embarrassed I immediately left the dance with my crew. We took the taxi home and for the rest of the night we talked about the Bore Nose Posse and the Bucca's Crew. We were taken aback by their name brand clothes and their ability to buy the most expensive liquor.

Yet another Guy

On my way home that Sunday evening, after an adventurous weekend, that Sunday evening as I returned home on the bus, I could not help but wonder, "Who was that guy that I was dancing with?" His voice was really coarse and he dressed like a bad boy with his handkerchief in his back pocket and a Bucca's hat on. He called me baby and I liked that. I remember when I was leaving the party after my cousin Patty rained on my parade, he whispered in my ears, "Come and check me at Connection." Then he added, "Ask for Vace if you do not see me on the front." Connection was a street that was joined to Jane Street and a lot of guys hung out at the front selling drugs, playing dominoes or smoking. I arrived home at about 6 pm and went straight to my room to call Jody and tell her about the new man that I met. I told her my thoughts about him being a bad guy and that I was stepping up my game.

Monday afternoon, Jody and I decided to skip school and head to Jane and Connection. As soon as we got to the corner there was a group of bad men standing beside the plaza. I felt my hands sweating, I was so nervous. I was almost too nervous to even ask for Vace. So, Jody asked the men, "Does anyone know Vace?" A Rasta guy showed us, "Over there." I looked over, and there he was.

An exciting relationship developed between Vace and me, so I began travelling to Connection frequently. The intimate energy between us was awesome, however I had only been with him twice. Unfortunately, a month passed, and I did not see my period. I was not sure if I was pregnant, but it felt that way. I started reading about the symptoms although I already knew what they were. For the most part, I wanted to be pregnant because I did not want to get raped by my stepfather. I always dreaded, "What if he raped me one day and I got pregnant for him? What would happen to me?" I was still in school. Now it did not matter because I wanted to move out and just maybe that was my ticket to do so.

Eventually I took a pregnancy test, and it confirmed yes. I told Vace I was pregnant with his child, and he was the most excited man ever. He said he knew it. I did not know what he meant at the time, so I just went with what he said. He kept saying, "I'm going to have a Canadian baby. I want a boy," he continued. Vace was originally from Waterhouse in Jamaica which was known to be a bad area. He came to Canada illegally and quickly found a woman to marry so that he could get his landing. Yes, that's right, I was pregnant for a 26-year-old married man; but he said it was a paid marriage. He promised me that he was going to take care of me and my unborn baby. Unfortunately, when his wife found out that I was pregnant with his child she told him that the immigration said he had to return to Jamaica to get his landing paper. He left for Jamaica, promising me that he will return.

Living on my own

I was having severe morning sickness and missing a lot of school. My mother could not hide the pregnancy from my stepfather for too long and living there was not an option, so I applied for government housing. I started buying things that I would need for my apartment, and I got a lot of clothes packed away for my first baby. I hardly heard from Vace since he went to Jamaica. He would call but I did not want to talk to him. I wondered for some time if I would ever see him again. Fortunately, his brother became my best friend, and we began to hang out together.

Nevertheless, pregnancy did not stop me from stealing and I never got caught until one day I went to Sherway Garden. We had credit cards and we decided to use them in the Bay. My friends and I were standing at the corner, my stomach was big, trying to defraud the cashier when I saw the security coming towards us. I ran out of the store towards the parking lot, but the police were patrolling the place. I squeezed underneath the car to hide but then I saw a flashlight beaming at me under the car. I was arrested and my friend Marjorie had to bail me. Fortunately, I did not need to go to the courthouse, they simply gave me a pink form with my court papers.

The Second Baby father

After I had my first beautiful baby boy, I was at my mother's for about three months before I moved into my apartment at Markham and Ellesmere. Mother gave me her bedroom set and I felt elated about having my own place, it was kept really neat and clean. Tayvon, the baby had his own room, but I kept him in mine as it was just the two of us. After a while Tayvon started spending a lot of time at mother's, especially when I was partying. I would knock on my mother's door, push him inside the house as soon as she opened the door and run back into the taxi. My mother loved Tayvon, he was her first grandson, but sometimes she wanted a break. My sister also loved him and always wanted him to be at the house. Tayvon was now two years old and Vace had still not returned to Canada, but he was very vocal telling me that I had better not have a boyfriend or bring any man close to his son.

However, I did not listen to Vace. One night Jody invited me to a dance in Glendora and I met Lucini, my second baby father. We exchanged phone numbers and began conversing shortly after. He was a tall, light skinned, mixed black Chinese man and as we got to know more about each other, I realized that he was a gangster; he and his crew did not play. Soon after we started dating, I began having morning sickness. I called Lucini, at the time he was in Montreal, and told him that I was pregnant, he simply said, "That is very good." It seemed as though he really loved children, so I wanted to have his baby. I spent the weekend in Montreal with Lucini and his crew; we went to a stage show. At the entrance they were conducting a search which meant I had to carry his gun between my legs into the show. While staying in Montreal, Lucini moved me to another apartment where this young lady lived with her baby. Surprisingly after leaving Montreal, I found out that the young lady at the apartment was Lucini's baby mother, but the plot would thicken. He lived with another baby mother who had five or six children and to add insult to injury I was his 13th.

When I confronted him about all that I heard he admitted everything but simply laughed about it. Following the confrontation, I spent the entire day locked up in my room in the dark, I only came out to feed Tayvon. When I looked at Tayvon I was excited that he would have someone to play with as he seemed lonely. I think that was one of the main reasons I kept my baby after hearing the horrific news. However, I spoke to a few of my friends who suggested that I had an abortion. I thought about it, but I always remembered the Praise the Lord program I watched with Mama and what they said about abortion. As we watched the program the baby in the mother's womb kept on singing, "Let me live. Let me feel your arms around me. Let me live." I never forgot that song, so I opted against it. I really did not believe in abortion and never will. During my pregnancy I did not see Lucini much; he would call and check on me, but realistically, it was just me, Tayvon and my unborn baby.

Back on the Streets

I was back on the road but this time boosting became my profession. Boosting was where the clients would enter the stores to look at what they wanted, then I would skillfully get the particular items from the stores and charge the customers at half the price. I would call my new best friend Ike and ask, "Do you want to go on the road today?" Ike lived in the other building across from mine with his baby mother Cherry. Ike was a no-nonsense guy; he smiled a lot, but I did not let that fool me. I knew when he was quiet, he and Cherry had a fight about something; we really never talked much about his relationship.

Eventually Ike was more like my bodyguard, and I always felt safe with him around. One morning he came very early to my apartment for us to go out boosting. That day Ike, Tiny and I along with Senior, Tiny's boyfriend and also our driver, drove to different malls to get lots of clothes and sheets. After a successful venture we made one last stop; the car was packed with stolen goods. At the last stop, we split up to go into Warden Woods Mall. I was about seven months pregnant and was getting really heavy. After I did my bit, I stood outside the mall waiting for everyone when suddenly I saw Tiny running up on Ward Avenue with a security guard chasing her. Then I saw Ike exiting the mall with the security guy holding onto him. The police cars were right there; Ike and Tiny got caught and I got away...or so I thought.

I managed to return to my apartment, and I had the sudden urge to get rid of all the stolen goods; I had VCRs and electronic things under my bed. I followed my instinct and at about nine o' clock I heard someone pounding on my door. The knocking was getting harder and louder; I knew it was the

Metro Police. I heard them saying, "Yvonne Reid we know that you are in there, open the door or else we will be forced to kick it down." I finally opened the door, and the police treated me as though I was a big drug lord; they searched through my entire apartment while the neighbours gathered around and stared through my balcony. I started pretending like I was going crazy as I really wanted the police to leave. At that moment I was thinking that maybe I did not get rid of everything from my apartment and maybe they would find something and arrest me which would force me to leave my son. The police finally left because they could not find anything.

Following their departure, Tiny called me; she was scared as she thought the police would go to her house. The police did ask who the third party was but, in the projects, we never ratted (talked) on each other. It still remained a mystery how the police knew where I lived. Ike came out the next day; he got multiple charges for assaulting the security guard.

The time came for the baby to be born. The doctor told me that I had to go into the hospital within two weeks to induce labor for a Caesarian; C section. I did not worry about going by myself because I knew that Ike would be there with me. I never understood why Cherry never had a problem with me but later we became really good friends and that bond remained. Unfortunately, Ike ended up in prison for killing a man outside the apartment building.

Chapter 8
The Return of Vace

Rickie, Vace's brother, called to say he was coming to check on me. After Vace went back to Jamaica, Rickie ensured that my son and I were taken care of. He would take me around town when I did not have a ride. He did not fancy stealing because he could not make enough money from that; drugs were his thing, and he was serious about it. That night Rickie told me that his brother was returning to Canada within a few days, and he knew that I was pregnant; the thought of him seeing me pregnant was horrible. Vace always talked about me being his first baby mother, so I knew exactly how he was feeling when he heard that I was having a baby for another man; especially now that he had to face his friends in Connection. He spoke highly of me and always said that one day he was going to come back to me and our son. I told Richie I did not want to see him, but he said Vace told him he was coming home to me and my son, and it did not matter if I was pregnant with another man's child.

He wanted me back.

Vace came back the same week I was admitted and gave birth to Tayshaun, another beautiful and peaceful boy child. I came home from the hospital and my mother was there to help with my new baby because I had another c-section which was just so painful. When Tayshaun was about four months old Vace called to say he really wanted to see his son. However, I told him that it was too late hence he should come the next day.

 The truth was I really did not want to see him because he was coming with all the questions. 'Why didn't you wait for me? "How did you let a next man touch you?" The next morning, very early, I heard a knock at my apartment door, I knew it was Vace. I opened the door and he immediately rushed in and asked, "Where's my son?" He had only seen pictures of his child.

Tayvon was excited to see his father, he hugged and started jumping all over him; right there, I realized how much my son needed his father. I kept walking around the house trying to avoid him until he put Tayvon to sleep. He came into the kitchen where I was, hugged me so tightly and said "Baby, I miss you so much." I could not help the tears running down my face; that was a heartfelt moment, I wanted my baby father back. Not too long after, Vace moved back into my life. He worked hard to take care of us, he bought me what I needed, and he did not support me stealing. However, he was a very jealous man and did not like me going over my friends to hang out; After a while I got tired of him watching and nagging me about having another baby and he was not the father. I knew that trust was lost, and he was insecure. Additionally, he did not treat Tayshaun as he did his son, and I was not prepared to allow any of my sons to endure the trauma I experienced with my stepfather. Mama always says if you love the cow then you must love the calf as well. My boys meant everything to me, and I wanted them to be treated fairly.

The communities met

It was late Friday evening when Vace came in from work; his friend was organizing a big dance at Jane and Finch, and he was rather excited. I had not been to a party in a while, so I was looking forward to going. In order to be fully prepared for the party we went shopping at Yorkdale, one of the biggest malls in Toronto. There, Vace bought me a dress for $500 and a pair of shoes that was equally expensive. He liked nice things and loved when I was dressed up. An afternoon shortly before the party the boys and I were at home when my phone rang; it was Lucini, Tayshaun's father. "Wow what breeze blew you to call me?" I said. "How is my son?" he asked. "I want him to meet his other siblings," he continued. Based on his tone he knew that

Vace was back. "I am coming to see you," he demanded. I replied, "I don't think so, after all this time you want to see me?"

He started telling me that he did not want any man to be treating his son badly; I really did not know why he would say that. He went on to explain that he was going to call Vace and warn him; he was acting jealous. He continued "Yvonne, I want to see you. When can I see you?" he asked. "Not right now," I told him. "You're tripping and I am not about to fall with you", 'Why now, you have been doing your thing without us' I said. I told him to just leave me alone and go find his baby mothers.

After dinner that evening, Vace responded to a knock at the door; shortly after I heard him calling me. As I went towards the door, I saw Lucini standing in the living room. "Where's my boy?" "He's in his room," I replied. "Call him for me," he demanded. Lucini was not one to start a war, he was a rather quiet person and did not like it when I tried to start any kind of argument with him; but that was just a facade.

I looked over at Vace and he had this serious look on his face. In the twinkling of an eye, I was standing in the middle of my living room with my two baby fathers, one from Jane and Finch and the other from Village; the two opposing communities that were always at war. Was I thinking about this when I got involved with either of them? Not really.

Lucini had this coolness about him, you would never think that he was a gangster; but he and his crew were dangerous boys, no one played with them, they were hot heads. Vace, on the other hand, had a hoarse voice that could scare anyone, and he had this special walk. He was very "sneaking", so no one knew when he did anything; he talked about only what he wanted you to know. Both men came from rough areas in Jamaica and were blessed to make it out alive. In Canada they were no different; they 'hung out' in the projects. The evening went better than I thought it would; I thought there would be a shootout in my apartment. Like a cowboy movie. Lucini kept asking Tayshaun, "Are you okay, did anyone beat or treat you badly?" He told his dad no. When Lucini finally left, I was convinced he was upset about Vace living with me.

Things Got Ugly

I was truly getting tired of being lectured about giving away my body to another man and allowing another man to impregnate me. Vace went off that night, got angry, and I was just thanking God that everyone was alive. I did not answer him because he seemed like he would have slapped me. Vace had never hit me before, but that night I did not trust him, hence I closed my mouth and let him nag the hell out of me.

Finally, it was the night of the party; we left the kids at my mothers'. Tiny and her boyfriend were coming with us; we would drive in their car. I remember that night I saw myself in the mirror and felt like the most beautiful woman in the world; my name brand dress and shoes and my hairstyle were smashing. Vace kept admiring me, but I did not care that much for him anymore. My thoughts took me back a few months earlier. I had left him at the apartment and went on the road with my friends; Vace did not know that I returned home early that day. As I walked up the stairwell towards my apartment door, I had a gut feeling something was wrong. I heard Vace talking so instead of opening my apartment door, I opened the door towards the stairwell and there he was talking to a girl.

As I moved closer, I saw him leaning his body on a girl that I knew; he spotted me and they both ran off. I ran after them and grabbed the girl by the back of her neck; I was about to beat her, but she slipped out of my hand. Later that day she sent a message saying she did not know that Vace was my baby father. I did not care what she was sorry about because my intention was already in full effect; I wanted to beat her and teach her a lesson. Vace delayed coming home then called me from his mother's house acting as though he was not with the girl, and he did not know what I was talking about. I did not believe, hence I kept pressuring him, but he gave me a story saying he was just selling her some drugs. I could feel it, things were not the same anymore, our relationship was fading. I did not trust him, and I was at a place where I did not care about him or our life together.

The phone rang; it was Tiny and her boyfriend telling us to meet them downstairs. Everyone was going to the party because General Trees, a 'big' entertainer from Jamaica and also Vace's friend, would be there. General Trees and Vace lived in the same community; they were very good friends. When we finally got to the party it was a packed house. Fortunately, we found a corner to stand; Vace and Tiny's boyfriend went to buy something for us to drink, then Vace began walking around and checking all his friends. As I was looking around the dance, I saw about seven of Lucini's baby mothers. Shortly after I saw a group of men enter the party wearing long trench coats. Well look who is here I thought, my baby father Lucini and his crew; almost all eyes were on them. At that moment I did not care how many of his baby mothers were there, I considered myself **THE** baby mother. I was already told that I was number 13 but I sure was not going to be the unlucky one.

Around that time, I felt really tipsy from drinking, so I began moving my hips to the rhythm of some hard-core reggae music. Vace came over and asked me to go with him to meet the General, but I declined. I told him to go back and hang out with them. I had other plans.
While dancing, Lucini's friend Laffi moved towards me and said, "Lucini wants to see you," I looked around and did not see

Vace so I walked over to him. "I want to talk to you outside," he said. We stepped outside and ended up leaving the party to go to my apartment; that was crazy. I think both of us were crazy. I thought Vace would come home from the party to catch me in the house with Lucini so I locked the door with the chain. Lucini was strapped with his gun, so I definitely did not want him to walk in on us. The following morning Lucini left my apartment at about 3:00 a.m. and I took a shower then went to my bed. Shortly after, about 5:00 am, I heard Vace coming into the house; I closed my eyes and pretended I was sleeping. "Baby, baby…" He kept calling and shaking me. "Wake up!" "What? "I said, pretending that I was not feeling well. "Baby, people said you left the party with your other baby father, they were talking about it all night." I immediately started an argument with him because I did not want to hear anything else about it, more like a suicidal move." What are you talking about?" I started to lie, I continued "You ignored us at the party all night. You went to talk to your friends and totally forgot that I was there with you, so I left." The argument got so big that Vace left and went to his mother's, which was exactly what I wanted. I wanted to be alone that early morning. I had a man that cheated on me, but he wanted to be with me. Then I had another who just did not want to see me with any other man because I was one of his baby mothers, my life was confusing.

80

What!! Another baby?

A few months after that party something was going on with my body; I felt weak and nauseated, it could not be that I was pregnant. The last time I slept with Vace was about a day before the party and I slept with Lucini the night of the party. For sure I was pregnant, but I did not know which of the men was the father of my baby. I replayed the nights in my head many times trying to think which night I felt that my baby was conceived; it was crazy, but I was not about to give my baby a jacket (the wrong father).

Some months went by, and I heard that Vace found a new woman and I hated the fact that my baby father was with another woman. Whenever I called his phone, she came off with this dirty attitude like I have your man and you are not getting him back; she even told me not to call his number. Her attitude made me want him back just to prove to her that she was only the clutch to lean on because I was the mother of his first child. After a while I realized that Vace knew that the night of the party I left with Lucini. I tried to deny it many times but he was not a fool; he knew and it caused him to somewhat despise me.

The truth was we both had a lot of hurt inside for each other; he left me pregnant and went back to Jamaica and I did not know that he had a wife. I still questioned if the girl I caught him with on the staircase was in my apartment before I came and caught them on the stairs? I had a lot of things going through my mind and likewise I figured he had a lot of things going through his. I was also kept busy thinking about whose child I was carrying. I grew up hearing about a lot of women who gave their men jackets; a baby that was given to the wrong father. As a young girl, I did not know who my father was, and I did not want my baby to experience what I lived. One of the men was the father of my unborn child and if anyone asked, I vowed to tell him or her that I did not know at that moment. There was no shame to my game, I did not have anything to hide. It was what it was.

I woke up early one morning, called Vace and asked him for money for Tayvon and he told me to ask Lucini. I did not argue, I needed money, so I simply decided to go on the road with my friends and take some orders. After a successful day of boosting, Marianne's boyfriend came for me, Jody, and Karen- the car was packed with orders. We were tired, especially me, because I was eight months pregnant. We stopped at Eglington West to buy patties. As soon as I entered the Patty shop, I saw Vace and his new woman Sonica. She was a very tall, big built lady who had an angry look on her face; she stared at me, and I did the same. We were sending messages like we were ready to go at it then I shouted "Hey Vace, how are you here buying food for your woman, but you cannot give me money for your son?!" He called me a bitch, walked out the store and went inside the barber shop next door.

The Fight

My friends and I ordered food and drinks, but we wanted to start a war with Sonica who thought she was so tough; hence, I began shouting to my friends, "Let's leave the shop because this woman smells really awful. As I said those words Sonica rushed towards me, grabbed my neck, and started choking me while shouting "I'm going to kill that baby you're carrying, bitch!" "I'm going to kill you," I replied. I broke the pineapple champagne bottle I had in my hand and stabbed her in the face. However, she was a strong woman, and she was not about to stop. With all the commotion the customers began screaming and running from the store after which the owner yelled that he was going to call the police, so we took the fight outside where Sonica kept punching my stomach trying to hurt my baby.

Fortunately, Jody came out of nowhere and started beating her with a piece of board. Then we all found pieces of board on the sidewalk and decided to beat her. We were so determined to kill her that by the time we heard the sirens the police were almost actually on the spot. We scampered but as I tried to escape over the fence, one of the police officers literally dragged me off and handcuffed me.

In the midst of everything I saw Vace running from the barber shop in a state of shock as he kept shouting, "Where is my woman? Where is my woman?" His woman was lying on a stretcher with blood all over her face and clothes torn off her, while I was standing there eight months pregnant in handcuffs.

The police asked me my name and I started to give them a wrong name when I heard Vace saying, "Officer Officer she is a liar! Her name is Yvonne Reid! She's a liar and a thief!" He continued to tell the police and then I started yelling at him, "How about you tell them that you're not landed, and you're wanted by the police and the immigration?" Well, that did it, Vace quickly lost himself in the crowd. I was taken by the police to thirteen divisions. My mother saw the entire incident on the City Pulse News. Later my cousin Patty came and bailed me. I was charged for attempted murder, which was eventually reduced to assault and bodily harm.

However, that too was thrown out because my baby father kept his woman from bringing me to court. Unfortunately, life was never the same for Sonica; after the incident she lost her job because her brain was damaged. I remember after having my baby that we went to a party, and she was acting rather crazy with a butcher's knife threatening to kill us; after that I never heard anything about her again.

The Hideout

My apartment became busy with drugs, gun trafficking and stolen goods; I had a group of young boys living there. With all the activities that were taking place at the apartment it was quickly placed under police surveillance. Shortly thereafter the police came searching for Monkey, the leader of the gang. Monkey was a swift small body guy who always eluded the authorities. When the police came, he was hiding under my son's bed but when they asked about his whereabouts, I told them that I did not know who they were talking about.

However, Tayvon did not like Monkey, so he said to the police, "Mommy's lying, Monkey is under the bed." It was not funny, but I started laughing; the police threatened to arrest me. Monkey was arrested and I had to visit the courtroom a few times to bail him; I was like a gangsta mother to them. One of the boys, Omar, was very quiet and was always doing the cooking or cleaning and taking care of the house. There was a time that he did not come home for a few days; I did not know where he was until I saw his picture in the newspaper with the headline, "Scarborough Rapist." 'It couldn't be' I thought. I could not believe it, and still cannot to this day but it was his picture in the newspaper. I guess I was too young at the time because they said he was raping older women. I really do not know if it was true or a set up.

Delivery Time

It was time for my third c-section and none of my baby fathers were around. I talked to them but that was about it. My friend Marianne came to the hospital with me. After the necessary procedures, I had a bouncing baby boy. He cried a lot and wanted to be on my breast all the time. From the first moment I looked at him, I knew who his father was. Lucini showed up at the hospital, gave me a rose, walked over to the baby's incubator and without saying a word, he left. Oh well I thought he knew that the baby was not his but how many kids did he want anyway? Even though I wanted the baby to be Lucini's, because Vace and I were not on speaking terms, his aunt would not allow it. She was married to an obeah man and was convinced that I had put a spell on him; she also thought that my mother was an obeah woman. I was also told that Sonica and Lucini's aunts were desperately trying to hurt me, but I believed God would protect me although I was not serving Him.

I did not believe in Obeah but with all the childhood sufferings I had endured at that name, I hated those who were trying to use it to stop me. Now, with the baby being born all my doubts were settled, my son looked just like Vace and myself; he could not hide. When I came home from the hospital, all the boys had moved out of the apartment, and I was happy because I did not want all the guys at my house with my young baby. After a few months, I started selling drugs and we were making a lot of money which we used to buy gold chains with big pendants and expensive clothes for parties. We left the kids in Marianne's house and went to sell drugs in the lobby. Marianne had a friend named Trident who used to sell and traffic a lot of drugs from Toronto to Brooklyn, New York. Trident wanted us to travel with her to traffic drugs back to Canada.

Chapter 9
Getting Hooked

Trident went to Brooklyn New York to receive a shipment of drugs and I went with her. I never trafficked drugs, but I wanted to go for the trip. We drove to Brooklyn and arrived there about 4:00 am. I never liked the houses in New York, and I believed Canada was much cleaner than America. The next day we drove around shopping malls in Brooklyn; I was not familiar with the place hence I decided not to do any boosting.

The Pervert

We met with Beverly Marley, one of the famous boosters who was a professional at what she does. She made a buzzer or carrying bag from foil which was used to block the sensor thus preventing the buzzer on the clothes from going off. I was impressed and I wanted one of those bags because sometimes it was so difficult to take off the security tags in the stores and that bag would be perfect. I wanted to hang around with Beverly, she wore only name brand clothes and the best shoes. That night, Trident had plans for us to go out; she wanted me to meet her friend Devin and I did. He was a popular drug dealer that liked to hang out at the pool hall with his friends. He had lots of customers and would often leave to do business with them.

After the party, Devin asked me to go driving with him; I was feeling uncomfortable, but Trident told me he was cool. She told me how radical Devin was and that he had a lot of money, that caught my interest. While Devin and I were driving in his Benz and listening to music, he told me that he had to meet a client at a certain spot. We drove for almost two hours but of course the final destination was a hotel. Obviously, based on the way he danced with me earlier, holding and squeezing me tightly I knew what he wanted. I was not ready to have sex with this man, I just wanted to hang out with him.

We were out in the middle of nowhere, No Man's Land with a man carrying a magnum 45 "What could I say at that moment?" I said to him, "Well, baby, where are we, hon?" Right at that time, I had to be the sweetest thing. "Oh, honey," he said, "I just want to spend the night with you." 'But you never asked, dirt bag," I thought to myself. "Oh, I hear you, baby, but you know, we are here on some business, and I have to be somewhere early in the morning." He answered, "Baby, we won't stay long, I just want to give you a good time." " Dirty boy you're mad" I thought.

At that point I was completely turned off by that pervert. I did not care about his car or how much money he had, and his gun did not scare me either because I was already used to being around guns. When we got to the hotel room, he put his gun on the side table, went into the bathroom and I thought, "This guy's a fool, because you never leave your gun, especially around a stranger." I wanted to take the bullets out of the gun, but I was not sure if I knew how to do that. While he was in the bathroom, I thought to myself 'How in the hell am I going to get out of this one?" I had already decided that I did not even want a kiss from that negro, then he came out the bathroom in a G-string. "A G-string?! Wow." Then he said, "Baby, why are you still standing there? Go change and come to Papa." I thought, 'Papa, really?! You could never be my Papa.' "Honey, you look so good," I said. "But baby, I'm on my period and I'm so sorry, I can't do anything. "Baby that shouldn't stop you," he said. I wanted to vomit. I thought 'Dude, you don't even know me."

Then I cleared my throat and said, "Baby I promise that I will make it up to you." So, he picked up his 45, the gun, and went to the bathroom to get dressed. While he was in the bathroom I thought, "I should leave.' ``But where would I go?" When we were driving to the hotel all I saw were a lot of water and trees; I did not know where I was.

Cocaine

We did not talk on our return to Flatbush. Devin was mad, but I felt good. "Ew, never," I thought. I was ready to go home. We made it back to Trident and I was relieved; everything was set for us to return to Canada. Trident had the drugs hidden in the car, we drove off and after a while we made it through. We crossed the border to go back to Toronto and I was overjoyed when I could no longer see the American border behind me. We finally got home, and she took a small package of the raw powder with her into the house. I never tried cocaine before, so she showed me how they sniffed it. I placed some of it under my pinky fingernail and sniffed it, but I did not feel anything; I did not feel any kind of high. I tried it again and I felt a little buzz. That night, doing cocaine did nothing to me. A few days later I started selling cocaine but not the powder.

Trident also taught me how to cook it and turn it into crack. Shortly after the business took off. My apartment became busy with people knocking on my door late at nights for a high; luckily, most of the time, my boys were at my mother's. Over time I had a client that was spending a lot of money with me, especially when she got paid on Fridays. On Fridays I knew that I would not sleep because Brenda always came beating on my apartment door for crack. She was a single mother, a fairly slim white lady from the Jewish community but was now living in a two-bedroom apartment above. One night I said to her, "Why don't you just buy an ounce and smoke it for the night?" She told me that she could not do that because she would get too paranoid and think that the police were coming to bust her.

One day Brenda told me to just smoke a little of the crack in my cigarettes and it would keep me awake to make money. "Was this woman trying to turn me into a crack head or was she making some kind of sense?" I was not sure, but I took her advice, grounded the crack and put it inside my cigarette; that night was the first time I had ever smoked crack cocaine. The feeling, the ecstasy was like I was floating, so I had another cigarette loaded with crack and another one, and then another one. I could not believe it; just like that I was smoking crack. I thought that I had full control of my habit because I was still making my money; however, time would tell.

Marianne and I started partying in Rexdale at the Desire Club. We were now becoming popular. We were selling drugs and buying expensive clothes. We were making more money selling drugs than stealing and selling clothes.

Is He the One?

As the business continued to boom, Marianne met a new guy from Jamaica as a matter of fact it was an entire crew and she wanted me to meet one called Dave. With that expectation, we went to the party that night however, as soon as we got there, I lost Marianne's location, so I hung out at the bar drinking. I started moving to some slow songs while sipping on Hennessy. After some time, I saw Marianne and I was introduced to the guy who became my dance partner and later my husband. I liked him instantly, there was something about him. We danced most of that Sunday night and I decided right there and then that I wanted him... he moved into my apartment the following Tuesday. He did not come to stay but after being together for a couple of days I told him that he could remain with me until he was ready to go back to Jamaica.

Fortunately, the boys were at my mother's, so it provided the perfect opportunity to do a lot of things with Dave. I even began teaching him how to drive. Unfortunately, the time came, and he had to return to Jamaica. When Dave left, I missed him; we were inseparable and now he was gone.
I promised Dave that I would help him to come back to Canada. I paid an event promoter, but she had to wait for the right time to move him through immigration from Jamaica and back to Canada. Dave and I spoke a lot over the phone. I was making a lot of money; both Marianne and I were wearing the best and living life in the fast lane. Marianne's man did not return to

Jamaica so he was always hanging around with us selling drugs and making money, but I was really hoping Dave would hurry and return to Canada; I missed everything about him. He was full of vibes, I missed him just making love to me, us dancing and laughing together. Many times, I spoke to him I heard his frustration, but I wondered, "Did he really miss me, or did he just want to return to Canada?'

While I thought about Dave and all the money I was earning, the truth is the nightlife was getting overwhelming plus I had my kids to take care of. However, I could not stop. I had to sell drugs at night because that was when most of the addicts came out. Then on the weekend we had to attend the parties as we were getting famous.

On a particular night, Marianne, myself, and a crew of girls went to a party. As soon as we entered the dance the DJ spotted us and began calling our names. Immediately we walked over to DJ Short Man, and I said, "Please don't call us by our birth names anymore, call us the Gangsta Crew." Marianne and I lived life on the edge. After that night, wherever we went we were called the "Gangsta Crew."

A Taste of My Own Medicine

I never tried dating anyone else, I was waiting for Dave, but I was also getting addicted. I spent a lot of time hanging around drug dealers where Marianne lived; she did not know that I tried smoking crack. One night she visited my apartment to sell me some cocaine because I ran out of supplies, and I took the opportunity to introduce crack to Marianne. We went up to Brenda's house to sell that night and while we were there we started smoking "hula," that was what we called it when we put crushed crack inside our cigarettes and smoked it. That night placed me on a slippery slope. While I was selling to the addicts, I was also getting high and eventually addicted.

As a result, my supply started to quickly deplete. I was losing money and it was getting hard to restock. Marianne's new boyfriend who was living in my apartment would also sell a lot of cocaine, but he would hide it on the balcony should the police decide to bust the house; I knew because I realized that he was going out there more often than usual. One night, he left with some chick and believe it or not I smoked all of my supply. When the stock was finished, I went on the balcony and found one ounce of cocaine in an empty corn can. That night, I stopped smoking the cigarette and started smoking the pipe. I was getting so paranoid I began seeing ghosts in the house.

I also began thinking that there were snakes crawling on the floor, then it was big rats. I was smoking so hard until early in the morning I started walking around my hallway and knocking on my neighbors' doors with the crack pipe in my hands; I felt like I was going crazy. My brain was frozen from smoking crack all night; after a while I could not even find my apartment. I heard voices, I saw the police hiding on my balcony, I heard walkie talkies and something like people running towards my door. My paranoia had escalated to the highest illusion; my entire body was numb…I woke up in the hospital. I accidentally overdosed on one ounce of crack cocaine; that was a lot, a whole lot of crack. The doctor kept repeating that I was lucky to be alive; however, I was not interested in what he had to say; I only wanted to return to the rest of the crack that I did not smoke. I became a full crackhead. I stopped selling, all I thought about was smoking crack in pursuit of the high I had that particular night when I first smoked it.

Dave did not know what was happening to me, I kept it very discreet. One day Marianne called to say that some more guys were coming in from Jamaica. Immediately I called the promoter to verify if Dave was one of them. I did not get a favorable answer from her; maybe Dave should not return because I was a mess. I was smoking crack and my money was going down. How long was I going to hide it from him? Soon the call came, I had to collect Dave at the airport. I went to the airport, but he did not look the same. Well, for sure, I was not myself either. However, I tried my very best to cover up although I wondered if someone had told him that I was on crack. Another of Dave's friends was at the airport as well but his father was not there to collect him, so he had to live in my apartment for some time. We arrived home but that night making love with Dave was not the same; I still felt the frustration he had when he was in Jamaica but why? He was no longer there. I figured he knew something was going on. Dave had given me money for safekeeping, but I secretly used it to buy drugs. When he asked for it, I gave him some old Canadian bills and told him that was the new Canadian dollars.

He believed me because he just came from Jamaica. Well, one day Dave tried spending the money, but the store owner told him otherwise. As a result, when he came home, we got into an argument and Dave punched me in my face; I landed inside the closet. Our new house mate, Buzz Bunny, tried to stop him from beating me but he ignored and continued in his rage. I believe he was beating me out of frustration as he knocked me out cold. It seemed as though I was unconscious for a while as I woke up with a rag on my face.

It was obvious Dave thought that he was coming back to the woman he first met, the drug dealer that was really doing well or the booster that was making a lot of profit, but his woman became a druggie. A lot of times, I would give him all the excuses to go away to some crack house. Whenever I was in the crack houses smoking my new paranoia was that Dave was there hiding. I was always afraid that he was going to come out and hurt me.

One day, I was upstairs at Brenda's house smoking, and I thought Dave was watching me as I was lighting my crack on the crack pipe. No sooner than I puffed the smoke I felt a punch in the back of my head. Dave came out of nowhere and started beating me. There was blood all over and the other addicts started running for their lives. Things got so bad someone called the ambulance and once again I was admitted to the Centennial Hospital; however, I did not stay. I became so addicted that I just wanted to return to the crack house. Dave finally told me that he was going to leave; he could not be a part of my life any longer. Buzz Bunny also left; he did not like the abuse that I was going through. I guess the atmosphere was too toxic for them.

Chapter 10
Another Notch

Dave was gone, the boys were with my mother and my addiction had gotten worse. I was not able to turn over my supplies anymore. Every time I went to restock, I would smoke all the dope. My habit became expensive, so I started selling my furniture. Tiny my good friend was a drug dealer and she started to give me drugs on consignment even though she knew that I was an addict. When I did not have the money to repay, she told me that I owed for more than I had taken. After a while I was placed in Toronto West Detention for a few weeks. Most of the inmates on my range were crack addicts and although we were thoroughly searched; even our bottoms, the inmates were still able to smuggle drugs into the facility. However, I did not want any because that little supply was not able to give me the high that I wanted. On the contrary it would have led to frustration, plus just the thought of how it got into the jail was disgusting. Unfortunately, when I came out of jail Tiny took all my furniture because I owed her money and I also got evicted from Metro Housing.

I did not want to go to my mother's because I wanted to get high, therefore; I went to Crazy Sherry's house at Bram's. She told me that we were being watched by the police, but I figured that she was paranoid, so I ignored her until she started to hide the crack in her vagina; every time she took it out to smoke it was covered with blood. I felt so disgusted by her actions that I could not smoke. I eventually left her apartment, and I just did not feel the urge to smoke for a couple of weeks; later I discovered that I was pregnant with my fourth child.

Marriage at last

I went to live with Mama and my uncle Gin and Dave started visiting me again. I was still in love with him, so we decided to get married. However, Mama, my entire family and friends thought otherwise. Nevertheless, I had made up my mind, so I got married to Dave in my grandmother's apartment. She did not attend the wedding, but I heard her singing which meant she was mad. My schizophrenic uncle, my baby sister and a good friend of mine were the only ones at my wedding. After the ceremony, Dave could not stay at the house, so we slept at Cheryl's for the night.

Once, Dave was charged with gun and cocaine, but I was unable to bail him because I had criminal charges, so Cheryl did the honors. Cheryl and I were very good friends until Dave's friend secretly told me that they were having an affair. That very day my uncle and I went to her house with a machete; my uncle was very protective of me in Canada although he did not like me in Jamaica. When we got to Cheryl's house, we knocked on the door and she opened it but as soon as she saw my uncle she began running. My uncle chased her with the machete, but she escaped inside someone's apartment. In spite of all that I was going through with Dave, I just could not see myself without him.

Doing Drugs with Dave

Tamisha, my beautiful ten pounds baby girl, was born and I was now left with my fourth cesarean section. While in the Centenary Hospital I got a phone call from one of Dave's girls telling me that she was with him and that he did not want my baby or me; I lost it in the hospital. The doctors and nurses tried to calm me, but I just could not deal with the hurt anymore, it was getting too much plus I was feeling a lot of pain because of the surgery. I felt like my cut was going to burst open.

After leaving the hospital we lived at different locations until Dave and myself went to live at my grandmother's apartment; grandmother had moved to my aunty. However, living at 126 Bellamy was a nightmare. I relapsed on drugs, and I introduced Dave to crack because I did not want him to hurt me; misery loves company.

Now I had to support both our habits. I started ordering electronics from various department stores and sold them to the dealers to get drugs. While we tried to maintain our lifestyle, the kids were going back and forth to my apartment and mother's, but I knew that I really had to stop.

I realized Dave was acting strange; he wanted us to stop but I could not, and he was getting frustrated. One morning, 3 am to be exact, after getting drugs, the baby was in the crib sleeping and one of the boys was sleeping in his bunk bed when I suddenly heard the baby screaming. We ran into the room; she looked so scared, and I felt like something was wrong. We managed to put her back to sleep and Dave said we should go to our bed, but I did not want to. My body felt shaky as if I was going to collapse and I desperately needed a hit, I wanted to smoke more drugs. We called it " josing" when we got that excessive craving and pain in our stomachs.

Dave could not take it; he punched me in my face, and I ran into the bathroom; however, he ran behind me and started slamming my head on the wall in the shower. My head started bleeding but that was not enough. He said that he was going to kill me with the hammer, so he ran into the kitchen. I heard him frantically pulling out the drawers as he searched for the hammer. In that instant my son ran into the bathroom crying and I heard my baby crying in the room. I quickly grabbed both of them and ran through the door and down the stairs without looking back, all the time wishing that he was not behind me. I did not know what floor I was on until I reached the bottom, and I ran outside the apartment building. My only desire was to save my children and myself so I dashed into the garden at the side of the building; I begged my son not to cry else Dave was going to hurt us and I rocked my baby so that she would not make any noise. I saw Dave through the trees standing at the front of the apartment building with the hammer in his hands, after a few minutes he left and went back inside. That night I was one hundred percent sure that the death angel passed over me. It was not yet my time.

Rescuing Mother...Dave Left

Dave went inside and immediately I saw a taxi dropping off a passenger. I ran to the car and told the driver what was going on and he agreed to take me to my mother's house in

Empringham. After moving in with my mother I found out that I was pregnant with my fifth child; that was my miracle baby. When I went to do my regular check, the doctor told me that I was unable to have any more cesarean sections and that I had to have an abortion, but I kept my baby Tanaka. I went through great hurt and hardship with her but despite all the problems things started to change.

Eventually, I had to move from my mother's house because both my uncle and I were charged for stabbing her boyfriend; we heard him beating her. One night as I walked to her room door, I heard her crying and begging him to stop so I rushed into the room just in time to see Rank, my mother's boyfriend, holding her by the neck and choking her; that was when I lost it. I dashed to the kitchen, got a knife, ran back to the room, and stabbed him in the back of his shoulder. That was when my uncle came running up the stairs with the machete.

Rank ran but my uncle chased and chopped him in the head; my uncle had mental challenges and was triggered by screaming and crying. When we got to the police station, I heard him telling the police that I was the one that chopped Rank. However, I forgave him because he did not know what he was talking about; he was just scared of the police. Thankfully, the charges were later dropped after going through the courts.

After a while, I decided to give Dave another chance. He, the children and I moved into our new upper-level house. Things were changing. I got some beautiful furniture for the house and a huge tank with the most beautiful fishes; I enjoyed watching them swim and so did everyone else in the house.

As we settled in, we felt comfortable and thought it fit to have a Barbecue; people from all over came. While we were there, Dave got into an argument with one of my friends and she started telling me, in front of the crowd, that he was mad at her because she would not sleep with him. My girlfriend was not afraid of anyone but what surprised me was that she was "up in his face" and I did not see him try to push or hit her; How quickly he would have hit me if I were acting in that manner.

After everyone left, we got into an argument because I felt so ashamed. We started fighting and he kicked and punched me in my face. While I was trying to run from him, I fell on my neighbor's lawn and although she came out yelling at him he kept on kicking me. Hence, she went back into her house to call the police and the ambulance. I was so severely abused. I developed complications which forced me to stay in the hospital until my baby was born. A week after I came home from the hospital, I got a phone call from the AT&T operator asking if I would take a collect call from Dave. He was in New York City and I knew right there and then that He was gone. I started crying because I thought things were good. He was so good with the kids, and we had promised not to fight anymore. We decided that we were going to get help and once again my world was shattered.

As my instincts proved Dave remained in America and it was not long after that I started driving to Syracuse NewYork with my baby girl in the back of the car. Going on that long journey just to see a man that was running away from me, and his family did not make sense; however, I just did not know how to let him go.

I did not want to admit it, but I felt lost without Dave. Every day I thought that one day things would get better between us; I had hope that he would change, and we would have the best life. After some time, things started getting rough for him in America and I eventually had to smuggle his clothes and items back to Canada.

That afternoon at the Canadian border I was hassled by the immigration for hours. I had Dave's original passport hidden on me while he was on a plane with false documents. I was so nervous, but I tried to hold my composure. I finally got released and made it to Scarborough. Later that evening Dave came back home.

Back in Church

There I was again trying to make a better life. Therefore in 1994 I decided to go back to church and also start Ontario Bible

College. For the first time in so many years it felt like everything was falling into place. At church, I was involved in seminars and many other activities. Dave and all the children attended church as well and they participated in different activities. For the first time I really felt like we were a family. Maybe Dave's experience in America had changed him into a real husband and a father; I started seeing some good traits. I was enjoying Bible College and Dave was proud of me. After class sometimes I went walking to a nearby ravine where I would talk to God. Life was going well; however, I felt that something was wrong.

Complete Heartbreak

I thought Dave was going to get baptized. I really wanted him to because I believed that would have changed a lot of things for us. I started the Sunshine Club for children in my apartment and a lot of young kids from the building attended in the evenings after school. Dave and I spent quality time with the kids. We had special dinner nights and at other times we would watch movies or cook until I found out that Dave was sleeping with a young lady on the lower floor of our apartment. I was so hurt once again; I tried to be the best wife. At that moment, my heart belonged to Dave; I tried to do everything to please him. I was totally in love with him from the day that I met him. I felt that I had put him through so much with my drug addiction and I was always trying to make up for it. However, how much more could I have taken? I was working, going to church, going to Bible College, and forming the kids club. What more did this man want from me? He said that he loved me and the children, but his actions showed differently.

When I found out about the affair I went to where my "matey" lived – that is what they call someone who is having an affair with your husband. Basically, I was going to tell her mother and father that she was sleeping with my husband. Unfortunately, she was not home, but her parents stood at the door, looking at me as if they never knew that their Christian daughter was an adulterous woman. Following the incident my faith began to weaken. My attendance at Bible College declined until I dropped out and my church attendance was the same. People were calling me from church, but I would ignore their messages.

My husband did not stop there. One day I took the kids to visit my mother and on our return home, I saw fire trucks and ambulances outside of our apartment. There was a blackout in the entire building; I kept calling my husband but there was no answer. Someone with a flashlight offered to accompany me and the children to our floor. On our way up, we saw my husband and a young lady holding hands coming down the stairs. When he saw that I was with the children he started running. I turned and ran behind him yelling his name, but he kept on running. After the electricity returned, I ran to the parking lot and my car was gone. I started crying. That night I was so broken at the thought of a woman in my bed, and now in my car with my husband. What was I doing wrong? I just could not understand; but I was done.

I went back to my apartment; the return trip in the elevator felt like the longest I have ever been on. I got to the apartment and saw my children looking at me and I knew that they were tired. Dave did not come home that night and when he finally called, he denied everything. He denied that he was the one running down the stairs; he just denied the whole thing.

One of our next-door neighbors came over; she was tired of my life too. My pain...my complaints... she was tired of hearing about it all. She was fed up with what was happening to me and especially my children. She told me that I needed to end my marriage with Dave for the sake of my children. However, she knew that if I called the police and told them all the things that he had done he would be deported to Jamaica.

I continued thinking about my bed, the car, and the girl but I still could not call the police. He came home after a couple of days, and we got into an argument because the hurt was still present. He started punching me in my face and I was bleeding, but I was too emotionally hurt to feel the pain. He smashed my figurine collection in my cabinet and then he locked me in my room. I could not escape because he locked me from the outside, I could only scream.

Immediately my neighbor came knocking on the door really hard and shouted that she was going to call the police which made him ran leaving the house. I knew where he was staying, and I told my neighbor. The next day at 2 pm I got a call from the police asking me to come and identify Dave. I was so scared to go downstairs; I did not know how to confront him or say to the police that he was the one because I knew exactly what would happen. With all the thoughts swirling around in my head, I went downstairs and there was Dave sitting in the back of the police cruiser. "Mrs. Reid, is this your husband?" The police asked. I did not respond. The police asked again, "Mrs. Reid! Is this your husband who did THAT to your face? Is this your husband that punched you and gave you that mark?" The police were just pressing it in because my reaction proved he was the one. Again, the police asked, "Is this the man that did you like that? Is this the man that abused you in front of your children?" "Yes officer," I said, "it's him." I watched as the police car drove away and I just stood there.

What was coming next? I just did not want to stay at the apartment anymore. I did not want to sleep in my bed, so I took my kids and signed into a shelter for abused women. I rang the doorbell at Emily Stowe Shelter, and I heard somebody on the other side of the floor asking, "How can we help you?" I said with tears flowing down my face "I am running for my life." I guess she saw us on the camera, so she opened the door, pulled me and my five children inside and gave us a one room with a bunk bed for the boys. After six months of being in the shelter, I started going to church again.

Giving Comfort

My spiritual mother prayed with me and encouraged my spirit. A few weeks before Christmas I heard my name being called on the shelter's intercom to go down to the office; I was then told that they found a four-bedroom place for me and my children. I was so excited as we would spend Christmas in our own home. By then Dave had been deported to Jamaica.

One night before leaving the shelter, a beautiful young black lady entered with only the clothes on her back. Her husband took her from Jamaica to Canada, but he limited her clothes, took away her passport and all of her IDs. He packed away her clothes, and she could only wear that which he permitted. She could not leave the house without his permission, one day she tried and after finding out he took away all her clothes.

Fortunately, someone told her about the shelter, and she decided to run away while he was sleeping. She came to the shelter with just a blanket wrapped around her. That night we all surrounded and comforted her. We told her not to go back but she only stayed for a few days and went back; later the news came that her husband had killed her. There were enough of those stories in the shelter that should make one wiser or continue to be a fool. I learned that no one changes without getting the help that they need to change. That beautiful lady told me "He is a changed man; he'll never treat me badly again." She believed it because that's what he told her. She believed it straight to her grave.

Home at Last

I finally moved into my new home and got the children settled in; we had a wonderful Christmas together. I loved my new Metro housing townhouse, there were only eleven units in a very quiet neighborhood. My children were happy, and it showed. Not long after we moved in, Mama came to live with us; having her help in raising my children was great. Soon after we moved in, I went for a job interview at IBM Canada, a telemarketing company. There were so many people lined up for the few positions being offered, no wonder I was shocked when I not only got the second interview but was hired. I went to work during the week and partied on the weekend. At work I met Cam and she moved into my house. Cam and I went to the parties together where we met some other guys; one of which liked her. After work we would hang out on Bleecker Street with Blaze, Cam's admirer, Marianne, and myself. Blaze was like a big brother to me and so we always hang out. My life in church completely faded away as I was reunited with the party life.

This Love is Different

We went to another project without Blaze and the crew one night; and I met Paul. I really liked Paul, so I gave him my phone number. We began talking via the telephone and after some time we were attending basement parties together. After one particular party while hanging out and making a lot of jokes, Paul said that girls like us gave him the scare. He believed that we were bad girls, and he would not want to be in a relationship with me because other men would shoot him. I heard what he said but I knew he was feeling the same way that I was feeling. We liked each other, at least I liked him. There was something different about Paul, everyone called him TV. He had vitiligo; half of his face was white and the other black but that did not change how I felt about him; he was special to me. I remember the first time he came to my house my children kept staring at his face and my grandmother went to her room. I asked my grandmother why she went to her room, and she said she thought a ghost came into the house. I felt badly that my grandmother said that about him and I was praying that he did not hear because he was downstairs. Our relationship took on an intimate note and I loved waking up beside Paul. I watched him while he slept and just kissed him all over his face; he was so handsome on both sides. Eventually my grandmother started to like him, and he became her favorite and also mine.

One day I got a strange phone call, and I realized that Paul was not single; he lived with his baby mother who was calling to curse me out. Paul had told me that they were no longer seeing each other because she treated him badly and that I was the first woman who treated him so well. He told me that he did not want to lose me. I figured she called because she did not think he would have found someone and moved on with his life. The call did not stop me from loving Paul in fact we became inseparable, or so I thought, one would never see Paul without Yvonne or the reverse; but Paul never felt secure with me. He was not convinced that I really wanted to be with him. One morning after a nice breakfast Paul left and never came back that evening. I called his phone a couple of times, and it rang without an answer. I started to worry about him because he had never done anything like that.

I felt a gut feeling to call his baby mother and I did. I asked her if Paul was at her house, and she said yes, he is right here. When I asked to speak to him, he did not care to speak via the phone.

I was devastated; Toni Braxton's "Unbreak My Heart" became my anthem; I just kept repeating the song. Following that day Paul returned my call however, I did not answer but he left a voice note lamenting that he cannot live without me, but he did not know how to walk away from his baby mother because he would never see his daughter again. I felt as though I could not go another night without my baby sleeping in my bed. I wanted Paul, he made me happy. We had the most laughter, candlelight dinners and bubble baths with champagne; we brought the love out of each other. I loved the way he would wrap his arms around me. We prayed and read the Bible together every night.

The way he laughed and the way I laughed when I was with him was priceless. My Grandmother's voice drowned my thoughts as she yelled, "Yvonne, Paul is on the phone, come and talk to him." Mama really loved Paul and she knew that I missed him. I could no longer hold my composure, so I picked up the phone and said, "Hello what's up?" I heard him say on the other end of the line, "Baby, I want to come home. I want you and I want to be with you. I started arguing with him, but he kept telling me how much he missed and loved me. He apologized a thousand times then I just gave in and asked,

"Baby, where are you?" He said he was at his mothers on Kennedy which was not far from me. I hung up the phone jumped in my car, and I drove to the building where he was staying; I saw him waiting for me outside. He came into the car and started kissing me; this was my man; our hearts were tied together.

Paul's baby mother called me and told me to come and get his clothes; she threatened to burn them, so Marianne, Paul and myself drove to her house for them. When we arrived, she threw the clothes outside and began cursing. Marianne and I were not afraid to curse her because we had our knives on us. I think she knew that if she came to the car we would have probably gotten locked up in jail because we were ready to fight. I drove away from the house with what I wanted - her baby father, my lover, my man. My life with Paul was about drinking and partying and after a while we started boosting really hard. I knew that Paul was not used to that lifestyle; however, he loved it. He was not the same person; the way he looked and dressed; he told me that I changed his life.

Chapter 11
The Escape

My children loved Paul but one night I got a call from my husband telling me that he was coming back to Canada. The week prior to the call I got a letter from Dave telling me how much he loves me and the children and that he wanted us to be a family again. He said that there was a lot of killing taking place in Jamaica and that someone wanted to end his life. Maybe he was just lying or maybe not but whatever his motive was I felt sorry for him, and I did not want him to die. Paul and I were still in love, but I did not see any future with him. Most of our time together was about partying and drinking to the point where he would get so drunk people wanted to beat him because of his behavior. One night while hosting a party at my home I noticed that Paul could not be found; I looked everywhere but he was gone. While searching we saw a couple fighting him on the front lawn; Marianne and I took them on. I began beating the husband and Marianne the wife. As the action continued, I heard my neighbor yelling out her window, "Yvonne, the police are coming. You're going to go to jail and leave your children behind! Stop Yvonne Stop!" she continued. We finally stopped. The party was over, and everyone had gone.

Doing the Crazy

Leaving Paul was the hardest relationship to end but it had to happen. Dave was back in the country but leaving Paul took some time. The things that we used to do like going walking along the beaches and collecting stones propelled me to ask myself, 'If I loved him why would I leave him?'. I never fully understood because I never met another man, at least not yet, to which I was so connected. Paul the man with the two faces, one side white and the other black was the love of my life. Whenever I thought about what we had, it made me smile. I would just text him a smiley face message to say I will never forget you even though we have moved on. I will love you forever.

After Paul and I separated my name changed; I was no longer "Gangsta Crew" I was Gangsta and a new lifestyle was born. We were not killing people, but we sold drugs, stole clothes, set up robberies and hung around the guns, jails and did even more crazy things. Now I was "Yvonne Gangsta." I was a part of a new crew, and everyone had their own name; Shelly Bless, Jody Mention, Pretty Cutie and Vonnie Goudas; we were the most loved, the most hated and most talked about. Everyone wanted to be a part of our crew, even the haters; we brought the hype to the parties and people were there just to see us have a good time. Additionally, we took frequent flights to Jamaica to the big dances where the British, American, and Canadian crews would all meet. The competition, the passion, the crews, the drinking, video cameras, popular DJs and dancers took partying to another level. My name Gangsta was mainly a party thing but then it started to attract the real goons, the area leaders, the killers. Someone once told me that your name has a lot to do with who you are.

The more I was called "Gangsta," the more I started to transform into that name; I was also attracted to the Gangsters. I wanted to know who the real killers were because I wanted to be around them. One afternoon I was invited to a barbeque at Eglington West in Toronto, Canada. I drove down with Pretty Cutie, and we were going to meet Shelly Bless there. As soon as we pulled into the parking lot, I had a feeling that I was going to meet someone.

The President

The barbecue was lit. We were all drinking, laughing, and dancing. From one end of the room, I saw someone staring at me and I began staring back with a seductive eye until he worked his way over to where I was standing. "Hey Gangsta, can I have your phone number? I want to get to know you." "Well, what's your name?" I asked. This guy was a little cutie, something about him I liked. Something was attracting me to him, but I did not know exactly what until he whispered softly into my ear, "Baby, I want to be your man." He still had not given me his name, but he continued, "I love your pretty brown skin and everything that comes with it." I was getting turned on but not much until I heard his name. "My name is President," he said. I had heard this name before; this guy was a real gangsta; a real G. However, I did not know all the information on him. I gave him my number then slipped away from him to get back to my crew. Shelly Bless came over to me and quietly asked, "Gangsta, do you know who that man is?" I said, "Not really." She said, 'his name is President, and he is dangerous.' She continued to tell me that he was a killer, and he certainly was not somebody to play with.

I did not understand why Shelly Bless was going on like that because her man Zig was notorious too. I guess this one was more dangerous; I did not know but I would find out later. Shelly Bless was one of my coolest friends, I always looked out for her; we were similar. We loved bad men, partying, and all the pretty name brand clothes. Shelly Bless was also quiet with an innocent look, but one should not be fooled by that; she never backed from a challenge, she was always ready to fight. She was my party partner. We drank hard, got drunk and into trouble. At one point, the haters started to post my picture on the web and spread rumors about me. I thought that I was going crazy when I saw my picture on social media. I never liked when my name was called on things but after a while, I gave them more things to talk about.

    I was even accused of sleeping with a popular dancehall man that died of aids. They wrote bad things about Shelly as well but that did not stop her, she would go to the dances and speak into the video camera which would cause the haters to hate her more. However, Shelly would respond, "you all hate me because I am cute, it is not my fault, go talk to your mother and leave me alone." We never let what the haters said stopped us from living our lives in the fast lane; the dangerous lane that is, living carelessly and not giving a hoot. However, Shelly was also the one to calm me although I did not listen most of the time. I behaved extremely outrageous and did not care who wanted to talk.

    The truth is I was turned on by what Shelly was telling me about President. The relationship started and besides being a bad man, he was super romantic. One night we were spending the night at a hotel. He slept with his gun under his pillow. I was sleeping so close to him, and I thought, "What if his gun goes off and shoots me in my head?" I continued thinking that I was not ready to die then I heard him talking in his sleep; he was fighting. It was as though somebody was coming to get him, and he was fighting for his life. I did not want to stay at the hotel anymore; the room felt bitterly cold like there was evil surrounding us. I felt fear moving in and I could not stay in that room. I woke him up and said, "President, I want to leave, baby I can't sleep here." We left the hotel, and I told him to leave me at Shelly' house because I did not want to go home. On our way to Shelly's, I started thinking about what was happening in that room and if all the evil was coming from the people that he had killed, if they had come to haunt him.

While we were lying in Shelly's spare room, we heard knocking at her door and as soon as President heard, he took out his gun. He always thought that someone was out to get him, but that knock was just my husband searching for me. My car was in the driveway so Shelly could not lie but she was nervous because she knew that President was not about to back down; he would shoot without any apology. However, I was not prepared to let him kill my husband, so I left.

The next weekend President invited me to a baby christening which I found out to be his baby. "Why would he invite me to his baby mother's event? Anyway, I called the crew, and we were ready to go to the party on Jane Street. We got to the party and his baby mother kept staring at me while he stood with us at the car. I felt uncomfortable so I kept telling President to go talk to his baby mother. "Why do you want to cause problems?" I asked him. "Do you want us to fight over you at this baby's christening so you can feel important?" The situation really started to feel weird, so I told Bless that I wanted to leave.

On my way home, after dropping off everyone, President called and asked, "Where are you?" I told him and he asked me to turn back and come get him. He sounded quiet so I turned back and went to the dark club in the basement where he was. He did not look right; something was wrong. "What's wrong?" I asked him. "I just killed someone," he said. "And I was just paid half the money." I thought to myself, "Why is he telling me his business, what does that have to do with me?" I wanted to be at the club without him, I did not want to go anywhere with him. I felt the same fear from the hotel came over me; I wanted a bad man not a killer, which sounded real stupid. He thought that telling me the things would amuse me but as I started looking into his eyes I needed out; he was a cold-hearted killer; he did not have any remorse. He sounded so cold; he was only concerned about not getting all the money for completing the job. I assumed it all came with the game. Someone had just died but all he wanted was to kill the other guy that had not paid him in full.

Complete Fear

My life had become one of complete fear. It felt like I was getting deeper and deeper into hell; I left the club without President and drove home shaking and feeling nervous; feeling that same fear that would not leave me from the hotel room, it sat on me. President was calling me, but I did not want to talk to him. I did not want to even answer the phone. I just wanted to be as far away from him as possible; before that night I had never felt death like that.

 I finally answered the phone and he said he wanted to see me. I asked him, "Why do you want to see me? Who did you kill this time?" Then he laughed and said, "Nobody, I just miss you." President was from off Maxfield Avenue Kingston, a bad area in Jamaica. He was well respected in his area, by the bad men, he took care of them, but he was also popular elsewhere.

He was wanted by police in Jamaica and America but was living in Canada at the time. I realized how wicked he was when he sent out a hit on me and Shelly Bless's head. He assigned his goons to kill us at the big yearly British Link up in Portmore Jamaica. The goons stopped at Zig, Shelly Bless' man in Jungle to get a spliff before they carried out their assignment. They told Zig that they were on their way to the dance to kill the two Canadian women, Yvonne Gangsta and Shelly Bless.

Zig said to them "You mad that's my woman and her friend". Once again death passed over. It was not our time to die.

Pretty Boy

I ended the relationship with President because I met Pretty Boy. Pretty Boy was a tall dark-skinned Jamaican from near Maxfield; He was younger than I was. His street never got along with President's, there was always rivalry going on. When President heard that I was with Pretty Boy he got my girlfriend Elisa pregnant. It bothered him that it did not bother me, but I did not even care about him getting her pregnant. She did not break any law; it was all a part of the game everyone was cheating, betraying, or killing each other. No feeling lost. I was on a high and I was not about to come down. I never spoke to Elisa again; we were not besties or anything, but trust was lost. It was the game, if you did not know how to play you would die of a broken heart or die physically.

My heart now belonged to Pretty Boy; I knew that he was really cute and that he really liked me. He liked to party and get drunk like I did but he had a baby mother in Jamaica that he really loved, and it bothered me that he was always thinking and talking about going back to Jamaica to her. Pretty boy lived in Reloridge, I met him after a day of boosting with my friend Keith Hype. We wanted to sell some of the clothes to make some money. As a result, Keith made the connection, and we were able to make some money. As the relationship got closer, I realized that he was always awake at nights making and selling crack cocaine. He was not a spendthrift; he saved his money to go back to Jamaica. The truth is Pretty Boy did not really know how to handle me, any time I was too loud and aggressive he used to get frustrated.

One night I went to see him, he was not at home, but his roommate opened the door and let me inside the apartment. I tried calling him without success and decided not to leave until he came home as I knew he was with another woman. While I waited, I took a knife out of the drawer in the kitchen and told myself that whenever he came through the door, I was going to stab him repeatedly. His roommate saw that I had a knife, and he ran out of the house. Pretty Boy called wondering where I was. He clearly knew that I was at his apartment, because his roommate told him that I was there waiting for him to return home. However, he did not come home, and I left.

Travelling to Jamaica

Pretty Boy got deported, and my crew, the Flavor Girls and myself started visiting Jamaica. He lived in Sunlight Street with his baby mother, and I was not pleased. I would go outside his house and call him out. I did not care if his baby mother was there because I was very popular in his neighborhood; the people would do anything for me, I was Gangsta. All of Pretty Boy's friends were gangsters, they never let their guard down and they never left me, they were like my bodyguards. Pretty Boy was quiet and very sweet, he never talked about anything that he did; he was one of the smart ones. Although he lived in the heart of the ghetto, he did not get involved unless he had to. The second time I went to visit Sunlight Street the Flavor Girls were there, they had their man in the street. I never stay in the lane. I rented a villa in Portmore, and I went partying in the night on Sunlight street where the gun shots would blaze like fire.

Almost every day we lost one of the men to gun violence or prison. There was always a drive-by shooting, so we were careful not to hang out on the front of the street.

Finding Daddy

I used to talk to Pretty Boy about not knowing my real father and he promised that he would help me find him. To honour his promise, Pretty Boy got his taxi driver to take us to the address in my passport, Lionel Town Clarendon Jamaica. We got to our destination and started asking people, "Do you know Mr. Reid?" We met the first Mr. Reid, a little Indian man who had lots of children. When he was asked if he had a daughter in Canada named Yvonne he said, "That could be." Right there we knew that he was not the man, I did not look anything like him. We journeyed to meet the next Mr. Reid that we heard about. As we got to the gate, we saw a young lady and I asked her if a Mr. Reid lived at that address and she said, "Yes, that's my dad." With that I proceeded to ask her if she had a sister in Canada and she said, "Yes, but I am not sure where." She also said that her family had been searching for that missing sister, but with no luck. Pretty Boy asked her, "Do you know this sister's name?" She said, "My sister's name is Yvonne Reid."

At that moment I took a deeper look at my sister, and she ran inside to call Papa. Papa came out and the second I introduced myself to him he started crying. I kept thanking Pretty Boy for helping me to find my father that day. He seemed happy to see me for the first time. After all, I was his first child. We talked until late that night then Pretty Boy and I left for Kingston. When we got back into the city, Pretty Boy decided to spend the night with me; he usually would not sleep outside of his home but when I came along things changed. I knew that he was happy for me and how he assisted in finding my father.

I told Pretty Boy that Flavour Girls and I were planning to go to one of the areas that we do not usually go to parties. He did not like us going down to that area because his turf and that area were always at war but that Tuesday night, we decided to break protocol and go to the party on the other side… It was a horrific night for us, the Flavor Girls and me. It was the night that we almost lost our lives.

Unchartered Territory

Although we needed drinks, the lineup for the bar was too long, so we headed to the restroom to perfect our makeup. We returned to the party and a guy, we later discovered was Ike, began showing interest in Juliet British. Ike was the area leader, he got whatever and whoever he wanted because he was the real big man; he called the shots. However, Juliet was not interested; his behavior was a total turn off, so she walked away and went to the bar. It was our turn to get liquor and the same man that was hitting on my friend was now serving. Immediately he started cursing us saying that we think we are better than other people. I realized what was about to happen and tried to calm everyone, but Juliet was not backing down; she kept cursing the man telling him how ugly he was. Ike took a bottle of beer and threw the contents of it in her face. Well Juliet was not having it; she grabbed a bottle and started wetting Ike.

I was now busy looking at the faces around me turning from angry to monsters and suddenly guns were pointing at us from every angle; I had to think quickly even in the chaos. Four men threw Juliet outside while others were standing behind me with guns in their hands. People were running from the bar looking scared for us. We had just disrespected the area leader; we should have been dead and there I was, face to face with Ike and his bodyguards. "Think quick Yvonne! Or else you're dead!" I told myself. "Oh my God," I said aloud. "I know I heard about you in a song." I continued, "I have always wanted to meet you. If she knew it, was you, she never would have done something like that. She is a fan of yours. We came here just to meet you and take pictures with you to take back to Canada; we are Canadians visiting the island." My language changed from Jamaican slang to proper Canadian English; 'like is she stupid, like honestly we are sorry handsome', and I continued going on "I swear this never would have happened if she knew who you were, we came to buy out your bar." I looked at the men that were around me and they were just waiting for his command to shoot us. Thankfully Ike's facial expression began changing so I continued saying things to make him feel like the don then it happened; he gave the guys behind the eye, as if to say, leave them alone.

I looked at Juliet and her wig was gone; she seemed scared because I knew somehow there was someone in front of us that wanted to make an example and get a name for himself by shooting us. However, the men relented, and I decided that it was time to get the hell out, so I bought a couple boxes of beers and left it at the bar for the goons. When we finally found each other, we quickly snuck outside the gate. As we were leaving, we heard someone saying "Ike's men are looking for the Canadians, to dust them" which meant they wanted to kill us. We quickly took a taxi waiting nearby and asked the driver to take us to Sunlight Street. The driver told us he did not drive to those locations, but he said he would leave us close by. While we were in the taxi the driver started telling us about the Canadians that disrespected the big man. He said that they were going to find them and kill them. I was sitting across from the driver, so I told him that I was from England, and for the remainder of the night I was speaking like Queen Elizabeth herself.

We arrived at Sunlight Light Street and told the men what happened to us and the look on their faces said it all; I remember Greg, one of the area leader, saying " Gangsta why you gone over Pink Lane " you should have been dead; someone shouted "you woman crazy " When everything was settled I got into an argument with Juliet British because she could have caused us to lose our lives and I would be blamed; I brought them to Jamaica. Vonnie Goudas called and informed me that we had to leave Jamaica right away because it was the talk of the town that Ike's men wanted us dead. It was far from over what had happened to Ike. For the rest of the month, we did not go to any party; we kept a low profile until we returned to Toronto, Canada.

Chapter 12
Are You Crazy?

We arrived at Toronto Pearson International Airport in one piece. My children were happy to see me, and, at that moment, I started feeling guilty about leaving them and going to Jamaica for months just to return to make more money for another trip. Travelling to Jamaica, spending, and partying at nights were extremely expensive; just keeping up our lifestyles was costly. I promised myself that the next time I would take them with me to make me feel better. I needed to slow down, but I did not know how. I was on a high and just was not ready to come down. The popularity and the drama had become my new life.

Hot Mondays

Hot Mondays was one of the biggest events. My friends Shelly Bless and Pretty Cutie started the event but after some time Pretty Cutie left. The event was the most talked about; every Monday night the club was fully packed. The event was so successful we had to move from Jane and Finch to Rexdale. We had a different crew at each location because certain gangs such as Bloods and Crips did not mix. However, it did not matter where I went; I was respected by all gangsters, they all knew or heard of me. Many of them called me "muma gangsta" - which means mama gangsta. Hot Mondays started to change locations a lot, either the club owner became scared because we attracted so much the gangs, or we needed a bigger location.

Married with lovers

I was still with my husband, but we lived in the fast lane; He did him, and I did me. I guess we knew that we were not faithful to each other, yet we were one of the famous couples in the dancehall community. We even went as far as winning the Best Couple trophy at one of the dances. When we were together, we did not see anyone else; our eyes were just for each other, every other lover was a secret. No one came near us; we partied like crazy. The dance floor was a big movie scene; we would be kissing all over each other while the crowd watched. Additionally, I would walk to the DJ's booth, take the microphone, and say "Let me send a shout out to Dave, the best lover in the world with the biggest penis. Immediately, all the females' eyes would pop.

There I was boasting about my husband showing him to other ladies and I was being cheated on left, right and center; a term my grandmother would use when things were happening all around you. Dave's cheating bothered me a little because no woman wants to know that her man is cheating, even if she cheated herself. Whenever I entered the dance, I knew exactly who was sleeping with my husband, I could see it on their faces, but they had to keep their mouth shut or he would embarrass them by saying "Hey gal do I know you?" and I would say, "Yeah, does he know you?"

I remember when I was pregnant with my husband's first child, he defended me against his lover. One day, while at Marianne's apartment, one of the neighbors told us that Dave was sleeping with Blade, a lady at the next building. Although I was in my last trimester, I did not care. We immediately rushed over to the apartment and knocked on the door. Blade answered her door, and I asked her if my husband was inside to which she responded, "none of your business." I went ballistic. I pushed her through her door, she landed in her house and there was my husband standing looking at both of us. I asked, "I guess this is where he has been hanging out?" He did not get to answer because Blade decided to attack me. Right then Dave hit her in the face and kicked her; she landed on her back. He kept asking her if she was crazy.

He told her never to touch me or else he would mess her up. I gave her two kicks of my own and left her place. As soon as Marianne and I were walking back to the next building the police came. Blade wanted to lock up Dave and myself. I did not know what happened with Dave's charges, but they were later dropped. I guess they made up.

Rasta

Hot Monday was getting very hot; I was so busy at the door one night collecting money, when I saw the cutest Rasta, he kept looking at me and I kept looking back. I knew that he was a gangster, and I was interested in him. We finally got introduced to each other, they called him Cousin. We started talking on the phone and Cousin attended all of my Hot Mondays. Our clubs never got shot up and the event always ran smoothly. One afternoon Cousin called me while I was driving on the highway, doing road; he wanted to see me. I decided to meet him at his apartment. As I entered, he pushed me against the door and started kissing me then he handed me a glass of Hypnotic, like he was planning for the occasion. After Cousin and I were finished, I followed him to the club to hide guns in the bathrooms. We dismantled the guards and hid them inside the bathroom stalls so that the security would not hassle him when he came to the entrance later in the night. Our relationship had to be kept a big secret because he was very private; he never talked much and was very observant. Only Shelly knew about our affair.

One day, a good friend of mine invited me to her daughter's wedding and there I was standing in the hall just to see Cousin walking down the aisle with my friend's daughter. Was I hurt? No, because I was not surprised. I was looking at him standing in front of the pastor, but we were talking with our eyes. I was saying, "Baby, you could have told me" I could almost hear him say, "That's cool my baby."

I did not stay for the reception, I tried my very best to avoid Cousin's calls and on Hot Mondays I would avoid him, but he never left me, he still stayed around. I believe that he had this high respect for me which made him feel that he always had to protect me.

The Night Life

Living the night life was mean, carefree, and dangerous. It was about 'me myself and I.' I did not care about hurting people; when you have experienced so much hurt it becomes the norm. I have proven that hurting people hurt others. Everyone was sharing or rotating lovers in the industry and it was the life. Men were robbing each other and shooting one another. Every night we went partying we were not certain if we would make it back home, but we were not thinking about that we were just about the hype. We were just living the life that we were used to, and we never feared it. We were a great big family, the Dancehall Fraternity.

Hot Mondays extended further into Rexdale. One night while I was at the gate collecting, someone came and told me that a crazy man was asking for me. The men at the party wanted to beat him and send him out of the club.

That was a special night for me; it was the release of my song "Gangsta" by me and Sample King. As I walked to see the crazy guy, I was shocked; it saw Backy, my teenage lover who took my virginity, threw my underwear in the tree, and left me standing on the street of Orpinton Rexdale in the middle of the night with no panties on and a broken heart. He was there standing in front of me, cracked out. Some of the men were insulting him and telling him to leave. I turned to them and told them that it was okay and that they were to leave him alone. I asked him what he wanted to drink, and he said a beer, so I got him a drink. He wanted me to dance and to the surprise of many I started dancing with him, even though he looked disgusting and some of his teeth were gone. He just really looked messed up, but I still danced with him. Many asked if I was crazy but if only, they knew. I could see it in his eyes that he was sorry for hurting me. I forgave him that night and after a while he disappeared.

Chapter 13
The Wild Ride

Hot Mondays was coming to an end; it was Shelly Bless' birthday, and she wanted to keep her party. Shelly's party was always big; she could not find a venue, so we decided to use the Hot Monday's location. That night was one of the biggest nights for Hot Mondays, the club was packed, and we were making money. The owner of the club smiled that night.

She is Dead

Cousin was not there but I figured he would probably drop by later. The party was getting really packed. The security had to close the door on those wanting to enter because it was now overcrowded, and people were entering without being searched. The security seemed very nervous, and my good vibes were changing; something there did not feel right. It felt like an explosion was about to go off. There were faces in the dance that I was not familiar with, but I kept quiet because I did not want to raise an alarm. Shelly was ready to cut her cake, so we all gathered at the table and started singing happy birthday, then it happened. I heard one gunshot then I heard multiple shots; the shots were connecting. Somebody was getting shot up and there were a lot of bullets. People started running and turning over tables to hide. I could not hide because I was frantically trying to find my son. I started shouting out, screaming over the noise in the dance. Then I kept hearing, "She's dead." That was when I went flat under a table. There were gunshots flying in the air and lodging in the walls over people's heads. Then the police came but by then everyone had disappeared; the club was empty, but everyone wanted to know what happened.

    The next day the police visited Shelly's house, but the news reporters got to my house before they did. "Everything happened so suddenly, I did not see anything." I told them, "We did not know the girl that died." They looked at me as if I were hiding something. When the police came in, I gave them the same story, "I didn't know it happened so fast." That was one of the worst times for Shelly and I, because that woman was a mother just as we are. We honestly never knew what happened; it was a mystery to us and so many stories were going around. Nothing of that nature had ever happened before on Hot Mondays. The security said that strange faces kept coming in and they could not control the gate at one point.

The End and the Beginning

Many people were trashing us even on some radio stations. The host thought that Hot Mondays, especially "Yvonne Gangsta" attracted gangs and promoted gun violence. He spoke about my name "Gangsta." I was not having it, so I called the radio station just to tell the host of the programme to keep our names out of his mouth. Surprisingly he interviewed me that night and I told him that my name 'Gangsta" never meant that I was going around killing people, but it was a party name. Like other artists who used gangster names as a promotional feed for their music.

I was not finished but Hot Mondays was. Every club we went to trying to keep the event we were met with roadblocks; I felt like the police issued something in the community warning the club owners against us holding the event. People also ratted out on us and told the police all kinds of lies about us.

With the death of Hot Mondays. Vonnie Goudas became my new boosting partner, and she seriously did not play. When she went to the store she did not stop until she got to move out most items without being seen. With the business booming we began packing barrels and shipped them to Jamaica where we would also travel to sell the goods. After a while Vonnie Goodas introduced me to the dancer, Shawty Versace. We began talking via the phone and he kept asking me, "When are you coming back to Jamaica? I want you to be my woman." After some time, I went back to Jamaica, Clarendon in particular, to get a little closer to my family. I stayed at my father's house; it was really nice meeting my brothers and sisters, and just getting acquainted. Unfortunately, later that year I lost one of my brothers to a dreadful bike accident. It was a very sad time for my newfound family. It was almost like they had lost my brother but gained me. I knew that Papa was my father but no matter how hard I tried to fit in, I felt awkward like I did not belong.

Shawty Versace

I met Shawty Versace on my second visit to Clarendon; he was my newfound love. We had a lot of things in common, especially the fact that we loved to party. Versace came with an entourage of men. We would go to the wharf to collect the barrels then sell the clothes; I did not have my own store so we would sell from the barrels. Word had already circulated that Shawty Versace's new lady was "Gangsta" and she was selling Canadian clothes which made it very popular for me to sell in the town. One night I was sitting on Shawty's veranda in Seven Roads Clarendon also known as Farm when a young man appeared out of nowhere. Shawty was sitting in the room on his phone. I thought I was going to get robbed right there but he asked me, "Are you Gangsta?" I replied, "No, I'm not" Then he said, "Who are you?" I said, "I'm just a friend of Shawty." He laughed and said, "Now I know that you are the real Gangsta;" that was one of the most notorious, most wanted killers in Jamaica at the time. He was hiding in the hills of Clarendon and came down at nights to get food or money.

I guess that night I was initiated because he wanted to meet me. He was surrounded by all the shooters. I was surrounded by killers, and they called me Mama Gangsta. Things were really getting serious. How did I get here?

The Stores

It was almost time for me to return to Canada and I needed a store to sell and keep all my goods safe. One day as it rained my sister, and I were driving when I saw a young man walking. My sister told me that he was one of the dancers, but I had not seen him before. I stopped the car and asked him his name. He said Crazy Squad and I told him that someday I would bring him to Canada to dance. He started laughing and said, "That's what everyone who comes here tells us. I don't believe you." That night he partied with us and became a part of the Shawty Dance Crew. Crazy told me that when I returned to Canada, he would search for a store in Clarendon so that on my next visit to Jamaica I would not be selling from barrels. I returned to Canada and started packing the goods to ship to Jamaica, but I was not hearing from Crazy about finding the store to rent. I called Shawty and he said since I left, he had not seen Crazy, but he gave me a phone number to contact him. I called the number a few times, but it was not Crazy; it was a deep-voiced gentleman who wanted to know who was calling his phone.

I asked him if it was Crazy's phone to which he answered no but he kept asking me questions trying to make a conversation with me. It seemed as though he was trying to make a move on me. I told him I had a boyfriend and apologized for calling his phone so many times, but he said, "I just built a plaza, and I'm renting units" that got my attention. He asked me if I was interested in renting, but I thought he was joking. He did not know Crazy, nor did he know with whom he was talking. Well, he realized that I did not believe him so he said that he would have his secretary call me the next day. Just with that I got my first boutique in a plaza near the Denbigh Hospital in Clarendon. I got the largest unit and even though it was outside of the town everyone shopped there; it was the talk about boutique.

People from all over the island came to shop. All the Dons brought their wives and baby mothers at The Fleur Boutique and Bounty Kids; named after the famous Jamaican artist. I was one of his biggest fans and he knew it. After a while I had two stores, things were getting big, and my business was flourishing but it was a lot. Packing barrels and boosting was getting more time consuming. I had to keep restocking the stores as workers would call telling me that the stock was going down. One morning, my partner and I decided to go out. We went to New Market because out of town was not as busy plus we were more known by securities in town. We went into the first department store and there was no one watching us. I decided to pull out my garbage bags. I filled one garbage bag with jeans, and I brought it to my car. I went back in and got the next bag and was about to leave when I heard them calling security on the intercom. I ran to the door and towards my car with two security guards chasing me.

One of them grabbed the garbage bag and I managed to jump in my car, but I could not close the door because the female security guard was holding onto it. I started the engine as I kept shouting at her to let go of my back door, she did not let go so I started pressing the gas and her feet were dragging on the pavement. I started moving a little faster and she began to scream at me to stop, then I slowed down, held onto the car door, and slammed it shut not realizing that her fingers were in the door. Again, she shouted at me to stop and I did. I opened the door, freed her fingers, and tried driving away. While I was trying to make my getaway, the other security attempted to pull me out of the car, so I had to use my wire cutter to stab him. In the midst of all that drama, Shelly Bless was nowhere to be found. I thought that they had gotten my license plate number and I was being followed by the police. I knew I was in trouble not only because blood was all over my car but because I had used a weapon on the security guard.

The Shooting

I returned to Scarborough really quickly and I called my children from the phone booth to find out if anyone came there for me. I also called Shelly Bless because I had to drive away and leave her in New Market. Fortunately, she got away too but she said she saw a lot of police cars and an ambulance going towards the scene. At that point I smelled trouble; I knew something bad had happened and to make matters worse at about 1 a.m. I heard a knocking on my door; it was a hard knock, and I knew it was the "boys" that was what we called the police. I did not want to answer because I thought that they were coming for me. However, I had to because the kids were in the house and the television was on. So, I went to open the door where the police asked if I was the mother of Taysean and I answered yes. "We have some bad news." I fell backward without saying anything; my entire body felt weak, and my ears were ringing. The only thought that was running through my head was that my son was dead. "Ma'am!!" the police continued slowly…. "Your son got shot, but he's alive, he's at the Scarborough hospital."

Immediately I grabbed my coat and ran through the door passed the police. I do not know how I drove to the hospital without crashing or how I got there. At the hospital I saw Taysean with a cast on his hand. He told me that earlier in the evening he and his friends decided to go to a barbeque around Markham Road. While he was at the party shots started firing and one lodged in the back of his hands; the doctor said it was close to his vein which could have made him paralyzed. So many things were happening to me at the time, I was not sure if Taysean was shot accidentally or what. I had to get out with my son, so I booked a ticket for both of us to leave the country; that was his first time going to Jamaica. I could tell that he was shaken up from getting shot, and so was I. I just wanted to get him out of the area. Tayshean had not seen his father for a long time, so I brought him to Papine Jamaica, in Kingston, where his father lived as I wanted them to build a relationship. At that time, I realized that I could have lost my son, but God gave him another chance to live so I wanted his father to be a part of his life.

After some time Tayshean went to Clarendon with me. However, when the gangsters saw his hand, because they heard he had been shot in Canada, they were furious. They wanted to be there when it happened. They kept asking my son if he knew who did it, but I was thinking, 'What if he knew who did it? 'What could they have done?" But then, you could never know because this is a small world and people have connections. However, Tayshean told them that it was a stray shot. In that instant they all gravitated to him, maybe because he did not talk too much and was always smiling.

Later that night the guys wanted us to party. That party was all about the gangsters and for most of the night gunshots were being fired, they also wanted Taysean to bust (fire) shots.

Everyone offered their guns, but he was not into the excitement, so he did not take them. I was also firing shots that night; it felt like some kind of therapy after my son got shot. I thought maybe after hearing all those gunshots, I would get rid of the fear of him getting shot again. The police entered the scene walking around with their guns but left in a second after getting paid not to lock down the party. However, they returned shortly after, I guess they wanted more money. Sometimes I could not tell the difference between some of the police and the bad men because they both were corrupt. I quickly realized that if you had money, you could get away with anything.

Nevertheless, I also learned the hard way that not all the police were corrupt.

Too Horny to Wait

One night about five cars filled with passengers left May Pen for a boat cruise party in Kingston. On our way back we got so drunk that everyone was racing. The breeze was blowing that early morning-Jamaica is a paradise full of fun. I felt frost (drunk), totally out of it. I asked everyone to leave the car Shawty and I were travelling in and then I told him that I wanted to have sex; he laughed because he knew that I was serious. I guess by now they knew that I was crazy. The men were taken aback with the fact that I could not wait. I heard when they said "Gangsta and Shawty are serious they are both in love." So yeah, we did it in the back of the car while the others waited outside for us to finish. 'Gangsta you no easy "they shouted from outside.

Chapter 14
Wanted

I was driving really fast when suddenly I came upon a major traffic jam. I refused to spend my time not knowing when the traffic built up would cease. Therefore, I drove on the side of the road, speeding past everyone while slipping in and out of the traffic. I heard police sirens behind me, but I did not stop. Other motorists signaled that the police were behind me, but I told them to tell the police where to go. I continued until I could not drive any further; the police chief blocked the road and told all of us to exit the car and that I was under arrest for reckless driving. I told the police that he could not lock me up because I had my money, and I would pay him. He told me that he did not want my money and I was very disrespectful; that early morning I was placed in the cell at the May Pen police station, and I realized then that I could not bribe every police officer.

The police at the parties kept on coming because they wanted more money; that was their way of harassing the promoters, but these were different ... or maybe if I did it privately, I could have succeeded but that morning I was very loud and very drunk. At the station I got one phone call. I telephoned my don and because of that I was out in a second.

My don bailed me out of jail but that was not my last run in with the law. One evening, Shawty came home and told me that he heard that I was wanted in Canada by the police; he said that they saw my picture somewhere. I did not believe him because no one called me and said anything but then how would they know that I had assaulted someone?

I was curious so I called someone in Canada, but I did not hear anything. Nobody saw my picture anywhere and after a few days I forgot about what Shawty told me. I was making money in the shop, so I decided to open a 24-hour restaurant called Roosters. Tayshean and I were set to leave in a few days; the restaurant was opened, and everything was in order. Now I had to return to Canada to not only steal things to restock the boutique but to get goods for the restaurant.

For the few days I had left in Jamaica I went to the market to shop for things to take to Canada. While shopping I saw a friend who told me that there was a warrant out for my arrest in Canada. She said my picture was all over the big department stores as I was wanted for theft and assault - bodily harm. Although the warrant was out, I had to go back because my store was running out of stock. I wondered if they were going to hold me at the airport, but it did not happen. We went through without any hassle from immigration or the police. The day after I returned home, I was in the kitchen cooking a big dinner because I had not seen the rest of the children for about a month. While cooking my oldest daughter told me that she had a dream the night before that two police officers came to the door and took me away; my daughter was a dreamer and I knew something was coming but just did not know what, so I told her not to worry everything will be okay.

Well, that same evening I heard my door knocking and I heard one of the kids at the door shouting that it was the police. Right there the police read me my rights, handcuffed me in front of the kids and told me that there was a warrant for my arrest. On my way to the New Market Police Station, I tried to imagine the look on my children's faces, and I felt really awful and somewhat ashamed because I saw my neighbors looking outside their windows while I walked to the police car with handcuffs on. I shouted back at them and told them to take care of my children.

Another Escape

I began praying. I knew the theft charge would not be so bad, but the assault and bodily harm would be. I did not want to promise God that I was not going to steal anymore because that was my way of living, so I just asked him to help me. We got to the station and the police placed me in the holding cell with a junky; we were both waiting for court the next day. They brought me food, but I gave it to the lady. In the morning they brought food and again I gave it to the lady; she seemed rather messed up. I guess that being in jail for her was home because she got three meals per day, but I did not want to eat because I was fasting; I figured that was the only way God would probably help me.

I knew that if those security guards from the mall came to my court hearing, that would have been it for me for a while; I would have to serve some time. That day in court no one showed up in the morning and the crown was not having it, so the judge asked the council to call the victims but when he did not get any of them, he had to put off my trial for a couple of months. Finally, my cousin came and bailed me out; she was always the one to come and bail me out of jail. When all was said and done, I beat my charges because the victims never showed up and there was nothing that the crown could have done for me to serve time, hence the judge gave me a conditional sentence.

A Chip off the Old Block

One would think that all those charges would have slowed me down but I was unafraid. I was packing and getting ready to go back to Jamaica this time with my daughter. I had barrels packed in the living room for the shipping company to collect.

One Sunday evening before I left for Jamaica, my girlfriend and I came off the road with goods to pack in the barrels, but I was greeted with the news that the neighborhood kids were robbing the convenience stores and McDonald's and my son, Traymar, was the leader. It was not hard for me to believe because we always thought that he was the mastermind of the family. I knew that something was up because he was always giving me lots and lots of phone cards to call Jamaica. Additionally, he had a lot of Nintendo systems that he said he got from his friend.

This is where parents should ask their kids, "Where are all these goods coming from?" But instead, we had to hide the goods in case the police came to the house. That Sunday evening while we were in the house packing, we heard the helicopters circling the neighborhood with its light beaming down into the backyards, specifically my backyard.

First, I thought it was us, that they were coming to bust the house for the goods that were being shipped to Jamaica, then I figured that they would not go through the back entry even though we had a lot of barrels with clothes and other items in the house. Then I heard my phone ringing. My younger daughter told me that Traymar was on the phone. She said, "Mommy! Hurry because he sounds like he is in trouble!" I grabbed the phone and asked him what was wrong, and he said that they were going to kill him. "Who is going to kill you?" and that was when he said, "the police." I did not know what to do, I was caught between a rock and a hard place, and I had to think fast, I had to go get my son. We decided that we had to go over to the other side of the complex because that was where he was. I hurriedly put on my wig, my slippers and asked my girlfriend and my daughter to accompany me.

While we were walking through the field police were everywhere. They stopped us and asked where we were going, and I told them that we had to pick up something from my coworker to take to work. The police believed our story and we were able to pass; shortly after I found the unit that my son was in. He had done a robbery, but it did not go as expected. The house that we were in was his friend's home, but his mother was hysterical; she demanded that everyone should leave the house, or she would call the police. Right there I lost it. I grabbed her by the neck and told her if she called the police, I would knock her out; she shook like a leaf. I was nervous too, but I had to get my son out of there and I was not about to let her stop me. I did not know what the police would have done but my imagination was going wild. I took my wig off and the nightgown that I was wearing and switched clothes with my son. At first, he did not want to put them on so I "went up" into his face and asked if he wanted the police to come inside and lock up his ass. Finally, he got dressed and looked like me; I put his clothes on and looked like him. I told Vonnie to take him and my daughter back into the field and over to my house. The plan worked because the police did not stop them while they were crossing through the field.

It was getting late and the woman in my son's friend's house wanted me to get out, so it was my turn to go through the field. I started walking in my son's jeans and baseball hat when I heard, "Don't move!" When the police came close, they realized that it was me, a woman dressed like a thug, so they allowed me to go. The next day though the police caught my son outside and told him that they found out what his mother did the night before, so they beat him and locked him up; later they came and kicked off my doors. However, by that time the barrels were gone, but there were a few things in the house that they took as evidence to put my son away because they hated the fact that we had tricked them the night before. They broke stuff in my house, turned things upside down and tried to arrest my other sons because they found money under one of my son's mattresses and said they also found crack cocaine. They took the money and the drugs but left my other son. The police told me that they knew that we were thieves, but they were not interested in arresting us; they wanted the boys. Traymar was in jail, and most of the neighborhood kids "ratted" him out, I guess because they were younger. He was not getting out of jail anytime soon because they had placed a lot of charges on him.

That was a very hard time in my life, I did not know how to handle what was happening to my son. I felt like I did not have any control because he was snatched out of my hands by the system. I was living a life that I knew was wrong, but I did not want out. I was not ready to walk away from it. Therefore, I always found ways of escaping the things I was facing, although I knew that it was not good for my life. I excelled at what I did and when the heat got hot, I took the girls and ran away to Jamaica. I drowned myself in my reckless lifestyle and I was drawing my children into it.

A Mother Figure

At eighteen years old Traymar got five years in a penitentiary. The hardest thing I have ever had to do was to visit him in prison, hence I hardly went. Instead, my mother would frequently visit the jail and later inform me about what was happening with my son. I remember writing and sending words of encouragement telling him that he was a soldier. He told me that he was doing courses and that he was Deejaying and hanging out in the studio. The years went by and Traymar not only came out of jail, but he took a turn for the better. I felt really terrible that I was a bad influence to my children and that I was not there for them when they needed me to be a positive role model in their lives. I was on a high and did not know how to come down.

I started travelling to Jamaica more often than usual. Lafleur's boutique my second store, became a very popular store; everyone came to buy their party clothes because they loved the fact that the Canadian clothes were different. The store was paying for itself which was good. I needed a change hence I decided that I no longer wanted to live on Sevens Road, Farm, I wanted to move from amongst the thugs; it was Shawty's idea for us to move. One night after leaving the store and going back to the car to pack and get stuff for the moving truck someone came inside the room and called Shawty; he went out and came back inside crying. He said that the thugs told him that he had to leave Farm now and I was not going with him; they blocked the road and said that I could not move out of the area.

After Shawty left without putting up a fight, I knew that those guys were not playing; they were serious about wanting me to stay and I had to think quickly. I was like their mother; I provided for them. I gave them money and took care of them.

One of the top killers came to the front of the house but he was not my type. Every time I looked at him, I saw death. I did not understand why he was in the yard because if he thought that he was going to replace Shawty he was crazy. He sent one of his boys to my room to tell me that he was in the yard and that he wanted me to come and talk to him. Obviously, I knew that I could not say no to that, so I gave the okay for him to come in; well, at least he was a gentleman. Now that he was standing in my room, he was so nervous I wanted to burst out laughing. Can you imagine that notorious killer standing in front of me sweating? I heard him stutter something under his breath. I was nervous too because I did not want that goon to even try to kiss me. He did not know that I was nervous because I did not show my emotions. I asked him to repeat what he said. He asked me if I was going to be his woman. He said that Shawty did not deserve to have me for his woman and that he would protect me.

I could not have told him "No way" because he probably would have just killed me right there. I had to think quickly so I told him that I would talk to him about it another day because I was feeling really tired from working at the store that day.
I held my breath and gave him a little kiss on his face. I thought that he was going to drop on the ground. He had this expression on his face like the "baddest" woman kissed me, like "Gangsta really kissed me." In that moment I handed him some money

and told him to buy some drinks for him and the other 'shotters.' I did not know how I was going to get out of it, but I did. Eventually I left Farm and moved into a residential area but that did not stop all the men from visiting my new house; those guys were like our sons.

They loved me because my name was Gangsta and like a mother I could relate to their bad habits and the things that they were doing. There were many times that I had to pay for funerals for the families who had lost their sons through gun violence. For many, they were living the gangster life because that was their way of surviving. Many of them were in and out of jail. I trusted only a few that were around me because I knew that they were killers who were always looking to rob and kill without any remorse or loyalty. I believe that they did not kill me because I took care of them. I always packed barrels of clothes for them, separate from the ones for the store. I also brought gold and silver chains for them to wear to parties. I also had my Don, the one who kept the community in check, led the gangs and sent out orders. Before I met my Don, I heard about him because he had a relationship with my friend. I heard so much about him that I badly wanted to meet him. As a result, Vonnie decided to introduce us. We went to his home after leaving the airport and there he was standing in front of his house, the most handsome cool dark-skinned man with a beautiful smile. Vonnie introduced us and from that day he became my Don.

Chapter 15
The Idol

Although the Don and I were never intimately involved, I visited all of his parties until I became a part of the clique. Vonnie and my Don were not close because he was married, and he also had another girl in the town; I became friends with her. After a while everyone knew how much I loved my Don and was protected by him. As a result, no one could rob my store and if they did, they would have to answer to him.

My Don became my idol. I felt like I was untouchable with him around and he placed value on my name "Gangsta." I remember being locked up one night and one phone call to my Don and I was out in a minute. I was hanging with the real thugs.

Things had gotten even more serious; it was no longer a dolly house. The police would come into big dances to harass him, and I would be in the middle telling the police to leave him alone. I did not care how many guns they had; I was ready to defend my don. I would look at his face and see how impressed he was with me for just standing there with him while some of his gangsters had taken off. I never left his side; at that time, I was willing to die for him if I had to.

The Change

As gangsters we liked to do gun salute at parties and also for the other thugs to know that we had our guns, and we had a lot. Every man was strapped; they all had guns. When we began firing our guns people ran because of fear. I figured if I were a gangster, I should have a gun and be shooting too; I became the only female firing shots in the dances. One night we were at a big dance, I was drinking but was not really drunk. Then MJ - one of my close thugs who went everywhere with me and was like my bodyguard took me outside the party that night and told me that if I were going to be a gangster that I had to shoot and kill someone. I took the gun from him and said, "Let's go." He brought me to the beach. It was pretty dark, but we could still see people walking pass or just coming out of the party to take a break. We saw this man leaving and walking towards us; we stood face to face with him, I held up the gun to his face and told him "Prepare to meet God" as I pulled the trigger at his face; the gun jammed.

The man froze and I pulled the trigger again this time he started peeing himself and the gun jammed allowing the man to escape; it was like a joke to me and MJ.

However, the next day I realized that I was turning into a monster; my attitude was changing. I was becoming more and more commanding and aggressive. My children looked at me and my face did not look the same. I felt like something was wrong with me; I was living a reckless life and I did not care. I never took the time to think, I did not care. I was on a role with no positive direction. I knew that I could die anytime.

"Shoot up" the House

Shawty and I reconnected and the love was still strong, we had an open relationship. I knew that he was a cheater, especially when I was away in Canada. I would hear about all the women he was sleeping with, but he never admitted to any of them. I told him I did not care what he did when I was not around, but he should not allow any woman to sleep in my bed; he promised me that he would never do such a thing. However, I liked him because he introduced me to many people, and they became my customers. We both attracted the crowd.

Again, I was in Canada packing barrels to send to Jamaica when a family member called and told me the dreaded news; Shawty had a woman staying in my house and sleeping in my bed.

Immediately, I thought, look at how much I was doing for this man, leaving him in a big house with comfortable furniture to enjoy, having a business and money coming in and that was how he was going to treat me? He promised me that he would never betray me by bringing a woman into my house, especially my bedroom set that I hustled to buy and paid so much to ship down to Jamaica. I was angry, a different kind of anger; the one that wanted someone dead, had taken me over... "One phone call," I thought, "and he is dead." I just did not care; I did not think twice. I made a call to Shawty and asked him if he had a woman in my house. He started to curse and asked me if I saw any woman; he was being sarcastic. Okay, so he was being rude with me. I ended the call and telephoned some of the gangsters. I told them to go to the house and tell Shawty to leave.

They said that he would not open the grill and he stopped answering my call. I was no longer angry; I was mad, so I told the gangsters "To shoot up my house." I told them to shoot him out of my house. I sent out the order and shortly after my neighbor in Jamaica called telling me to call the police because a barrage of shots was fired on the house and if Shawty did not escape through the back door he would have died.

When the gangsters left the house, my neighbor called saying that Shawty told her that I sent gunmen to kill him; I denied everything.

Shawty Forgave Me

I thought the relationship with Shawty was over, however, I went back to Jamaica, and he moved back home with me. Desperation is really a serious thing. I ordered the gangsters to fire shots at the house and there I was getting the windows and doors fixed from all the bullets, but I was hurt and that was why I did that insane thing. Nevertheless, I promised that I would not do such crazy things again.

My daughters were in Jamaica with me partying and enjoying the island, while helping at the shop. The thugs watched keenly over my daughters and treated them like their sisters, especially Marky. Marky was another one of the thugs that was close to me. Since I met him, he never left my side, he was my other bodyguard, hardcore and loyal to me. One evening after leaving the shop, Shawty told me that the 'shotters' were having a birthday party in the hills, and they wanted me and my daughters to join them. We decided that we would go.

Party Time

We got to the party and we saw the biggest, most beautiful house ever; the door locks and the furniture were made by Versace. The house looked like it was taken from a magazine. As I walked around the house, I noticed that the owner was living in the United Kingdom. This was where the Shotters hang out at nights, guns were all over the house. Everyone was drinking and smoking, and the music was loud. In one of the rooms there were two prostitutes and I watched as each of the men took turns going in and coming out laughing. While I scrutinized the house and got comfortable with Shawty and the shotters, my daughters were on the balcony with some of my goons protecting them. As we partied one of the men offered me a spliff, I stretched my hand to take it and Shawty shouted that I should not smoke; he always said I was not a good ganja smoker. Shawty said that when I smoked, I hallucinated; I would see things that were not real. However, I did not care to listen to him, so I took the spliff and started smoking.

After smoking the weed and drinking a beer I walked onto the balcony to get some fresh air and the bushes over on the mountainside seemed to move. I closed and opened my eyes, but the bushes were still moving. As a result, I went back into the house, and I called Shawty to the side and told him that I saw the bush moving; he started laughing loudly. He told the men that I said the bushes were moving and everyone started laughing. I was not laughing, I was serious, I got angry at the way they were all thinking that it was funny. I went back out on the balcony to double check and the bushes were still rattling. I told the men that it was time for us to head out because my daughters were tired; I had to find some kind of excuse to leave that house. Shawty did not want to leave and was upset about what I was saying, he still believed that I was acting weird because I smoked weed. Nevertheless, I did not care about what he was saying. I knew something was wrong and I needed to go.

Under Surveillance

The morning after the party I was in my office cleaning when one of my workers told me that Leather Shoes, a police officer, was outside and he wanted to see me. Leather shoes had coldness in his eyes. He was a bad police officer; he never talked, he was very observant and never trusted anyone. We had a little thing going on and it had nothing to do with love, but I needed him to be my extra protective shield. The only thing that turned me on was that he had a bad reputation; He did not shoot and miss.

After my worker left my office, he came barging in and threw his gun on my desk. He seemed angry as if he would hit me, so I enquired what was wrong. He answered and said he wanted to know what I was doing in the hills with my daughters. Well, I wanted to know how he knew that I was in the hills with my daughters in the first place. He told me that the big, beautiful house that I was hanging around and partying was under surveillance. The police were watching the house and on the night of the party they were going to invade the house and kill all the gangsters, but Leather Shoes saw me with my daughters standing on the balcony. I was standing there looking at him like, what the hell did I just hear? At that time, I knew I really saw the bushes rattling.

Everyone at the party that night was laughing at me without realizing that I saved their lives. He kept saying that they were all just about to run in when he looked up and saw me on the balcony. He said he had to call off the bust and the other police officers were not pleased about it. He kept asking me why I chose to be friends with all the killers. He said that those men were not worth it and that I could not trust them. He never trusted anyone so when he came to my house, he would check out all the men that he saw.

Church Time

I woke up one particular morning and felt frustrated; I was tired of partying, talking about who killed who and where the next party would be. Therefore, I told all the shotters that we were going to church the next day, Sunday. There was a Rasta in our crew who began complaining that he did not want to go to church. He thought that church people were wicked and just wanted people's money; but I convinced him to go. That Sunday morning, all the shotters were well dressed, most of them in dark glasses. Probably they thought that if the pastor looked into their eyes, he would have seen their wickedness.

We walked inside the church, and it was a sight to see, all eyes were on us. Based on their faces it was obvious that they were wondering where all those killers or thieves were going? However, some seemed pleased to see us. Nevertheless, what amazed me was when the pastor made the altar call, all the men were there crying, even me. However, did any of us change our lives after that day at the altar? Nope, not one, but something was planted in us; we started visiting churches, but we would leave and go partying.

The Chill Spot

We went to Salt River to party; it was one of the most beautiful places in Clarendon Jamaica. Many tourists would go and sit in the river for hours as they thought the waters brought healing. There are stories that people got healed from sicknesses in the water. Many parties took place on the banks of the Salt River. I had some romantic times, making love in the water or just simply feeling the natural healing water on my body. Salt River was the place for me even though I was not fond of alligators, which were seen in the river only at nights. Shawty was a swimmer and I always watched him swim like a fish because I could not.

We planned to go partying in Kingston later that night. Shawty was a skilled dancer; he always wanted the opportunity to go to a foreign country and dance; which was everyone's dream. That day at Salt River, I promised him that I would make him a star. We started partying more in Kingston and Shawty was getting more recognition for his dances. I was well known at the parties in town, many knew me as Gangsta but some just knew me as the lady from Canada who always threw away money in the dances or spoke on the microphone.

Chapter 16
Life Became Meaningless

We arrived at the dance at about five in the morning and we were just ready to party. The music was good, and I could feel the cool morning breeze coming from the nearby sea. The boys went to the bar and came back with bottles of Hennessey and beers, then the drinking and the hype began. That morning, I threw away money in the dance and the next day, while in the market, a lady approached me and said she was at the dance and from the money that I threw out she was able to collect some which she used to register her child in school. On hearing the testimony, I felt very good and wanted to do more to help the children. The truth is, I thought I was just throwing away money for the hype but hearing that story made me realize that there were so many people out there that needed help and just me doing that was helping somebody; I felt good about that and the fact that whenever they saw me coming, they would say there is Gangsta pointing at me. They looked at me as if I were a Hollywood star.

He died

Shawty's favorite dancer was Bogle, Jamaica's former dancehall dancer. They partied together at Ready Ready Wednesday and Pasa Pasa; those were the two biggest dance events in Jamaica at the time and the most famous places for us to party. We would arrive about 3 am and return home about 10 am; when everyone was heading for work, we were going to our beds.

I will never forget that night Bogle and his crew entered, they had some roosters, yep you heard me, they had some chicken in a basket. He was a very creative dancer and whatever moves he created they would later be hits in dancehall music videos all over the world. That night the heat was on, and the atmosphere did not feel right; you could almost tell that something bad was going to happen. As a result, we left Ready Ready and headed to Pasa Pasa, then we got the phone calls; Bogle got shot.

I was driving with Shelly Bless and Jodie; we went to the hospital and a few people were outside hanging around a pickup truck. As we walked towards the people, I saw Boysie and other dancers around the truck; it was a bad look. The dancer was just lying there in the back of the van until I heard everyone started screaming and crying.

I remember Boysie walking over to me; he seemed lost, then he said, "Gangsta, the dancer died." I just did not know what to say; all I knew was that a piece of dancehall was gone forever. That night we lost an icon. After Bogle died, dancers' riots started, houses were burnt, and people started to die.

Shawty's Big Break and Betrayal

I told Shawty that I knew Bogle personally and that he was the greatest dancer I ever knew but now that he was gone, it was Shawty's time to be the next great dancer. It was that time of the year for the Easter Dance Second Edition, one of Canada's biggest dances and I wanted Shawty to be the star of the dance. I spoke to the promoter who I knew well, and the deal was on for him to be the next famous dancer.

The first edition Bogle came to perform and at the second Shawty would be the big dancer. Shortly after the deal, Shawty and Crazy squad arrived in Canada a week before the Easter dance; they stayed at Vonnie's. After the dance, Shawty and his crew became popular; every promoter was calling for them. The next event was Camera Man Floyd's and he wanted Shawty to perform at his dance.

However, when I went to do business with Floyd, Shawty had already talked to him without saying anything to me. There I was thinking that I was the manager, but I guess not; Shawty was changing on me rapidly. When I was younger, my grandmother told me that men change like green lizards, from green to black, well, that was Shawty's behavior. He forgot that I was the one who brought him and his friends to Canada. He was getting money that I did not know about. I was the one dressing him in all the name brand clothes so that he could look dapper (good), but he allowed the hype to change him. At that time, it was obvious that he could not handle success and I could not handle betrayal and ungratefulness. I was being watched and talked about and I could not handle all of that; everyone wanted a piece of the dancers, and he was willing to share.

 It was the night before Shawty's return to Jamaica and I was furious at his attitude and how quickly he forgot who I was, so I did not go out with him. As a matter of fact, he did not want me to go out with him; there were too many women that wanted him, and he wanted all of them. I really did not think I existed in his world at that time hence I told him that I would stay and pack his suitcase because they were leaving early in the morning. While packing his suitcase the thought that was going through my mind was wicked. I could not think of anything good concerning Shawty, so I decided to repack his suitcase. I took out all the brand-new clothes and shoes that I got and placed them in a garbage bag and replaced them with the garbage that I took from all the neighbor's driveway. I decided that I was going to give him something to hype about. I kept thinking "who is this fool playing with me?" I was going to fix him.

Sweet Revenge

The next morning, even after packing the suitcase for him, he came home half an hour before his check in time; that meant that he was not coming directly from the dance. When he came through the door, I took my friend's glass vase and broke it over his head. I wanted to hurt him because I was hurting so badly but everyone jumped in because there was no time to fight or else, they would have missed the flight. He did not even have time to check his suitcase, which was good for me. I was satisfied, he "dissed" me, and I wanted revenge. I made a call to Jamaica and told the shotters to go to the house, take everything that belonged to Shawty and burn them. That day I waited for the suitcase to be checked in at the Pearson International Airport and then I left. Before I walked away, he said, "Babes aren't you going to give me a kiss?" "Oh, so now you want to kiss?" I thought. I gave him a big kiss and hugged him real tight. The kiss felt gross, I felt sick to my stomach because I knew that he was coming out of some woman's bed who could have been one of my enemies. "Goodbye baby." I said, "Call me later, when you reach home."

I went straight home after leaving the airport. No one knew what I did except Vonnie, and I laid in my bed waiting for the news. The first call was Vonnie asking me if I heard what happened at the airport. She said that the immigration officer had Shawty in custody because the smell that was coming out of his suitcase raised concern. She told me that he was crying then fainted. However, my heart was numb; I could not feel any hurt for that man. I was anticipating hearing what happened after he left the airport. Then I got the next phone call that gunmen went into the house and took out all of Shawty's belongings. The news of what I did was spreading like wildfire. The message was, "Don't play with Gangtsa" and that was exactly what I wanted to hear.

Another Reconciliation or not?

I took some time before going back to Jamaica. After everything that happened, I talked to Shawty via the phone, and he was still taking care of the shop and the house. Oftentimes I wondered, "Why does this man want to stick around?" I quickly realized that it was not really me but what I could offer. He was using me, but I was using him too; we needed each other to live the hype life. We were never loyal to each other and lived multiple lies but strangely we continued making sparkles. People wanted to be around us as we had vibes and we brought the hype to the parties. As a result, promoters were hiring Shawty to go to their parties. He was now on all the party flyers; where he went, the crowd went. Shawty started travelling to Canada frequently and I would hear all about the things he was doing when I was not around.

I was in Jamaica when he got a call to go to Canada to do a dance; it was okay because I had MJ and Marky with me. Also, we had our own chef and he never left me either. Shawty called me and told me that things were not good in Canada and that he missed me. However, he did not tell me that he was in a hotel with a girl until she called back the number cursing me out. All of my men were with me when that was going on. I tried calling back Shawty, but he did not answer until a few hours later; he was telling so many lies. He did not know what I was talking about, he claimed; the lies were getting to me but why did I care? I guess my reputation meant a lot to me.

Planning Shawty's Demise

I did not like when people talked badly about me even though they always did. Shawty was trying to disgrace me. The women that he was fooling around were below my standard and I was tired, so I planned that when he returned to Jamaica, I was going to meet him at the airport and burn him with acid. I told my friend Shelly Bless that I was going to buy acid and burn him because he was trying to tarnish my name and my reputation. However, she kept calling me to say that the Jamaican police at the airport would lock me up and that I would go to prison and leave my children but what I did not realize was that the guys around me were hearing and seeing what was going on with me. They always took on my "beef," problems, and everyone was upset. The more I kept talking the more upset they were getting.

    We were all at the shop when we heard Shawty and Crazy coming up the stairs. I heard him yelling about why I did not come to the airport to pick him up and I did not answer; after all the calls coming from Canada about his behavior, I was angry. Vonnie Goodas was there, and she had a little idea of what we were planning. When he approached me, I took off my shoes and busted his head, then all the men that were around me rushed him with knives. Luckily Shawty got away but Crazy got stabbed in the stomach and had to be rushed to the hospital. Due to the sudden attack they both had to leave their suitcases; we took them and left the shop. Word got out that the police were looking for me and the rest of the guys who were with me.

A few days later, Vonnie told me that she heard that I had a warrant at the airport so I would not be able to go back to Canada; the charges were serious, so I had to turn myself in.

Shawty said that he was going to make sure that the police put me away and the guys that were with me would have to figure out how to get out of that one. However, they made a deal with Shawty and Crazy so that their clothes and jewelry would be returned. Sometime later Shawty showed up and dropped the charges. At the station the police kept laughing at him and telling him that he allowed a woman to beat him up. It seemed as though we had buried the hatchet, but I knew that Shawty did not forgive me and that was confirmed when he took a Hennesy bottle and shattered it in my face while we were in the market. The splinters went into my eyes, and I could not see clearly.

None of the men were with me except the chef, it was a hot day, and I was bleeding heavily. Fortunately help came and rushed me to the hospital where I got stitches in my face. I did not expect that, but I knew something was coming. After I came out of the hospital, I went straight to see my Don and Shawty knew it; news went around quickly. The Don ordered Shawty to leave my house. At that moment Shawty called saying that he reported my Don and myself to the police. He said if anything happened to him, he told the police who would be the first suspects. Things were getting serious, and I needed to slow down and look into my life.

Another Death?

Shawty and I reconciled and acted as if nothing happened. We started partying with Vonnie Goodas, Shelly Bless and Pretty Cutie who would visit May pen. The shotters around us were dying quickly; it was almost like I had a picture with all of them and every time I looked at it one of them would be missing. I had a lot of men around me but there were a few I kept really close to me; one was Marky. My plan was to take him to Canada and give him a new life. He was like a son to me, and my daughters took him as their brother. However, he had a friend who came out of jail and wanted him to rob and kill me. I knew that there was something about his friend that I did not trust; he was always scrutinizing the shop. He never laughed much, and I just did not like him. He seemed hungry and desperate like he was haunted and was just waiting for something to happen. When I did not see him at the shop I asked, and Marky told me his plans. He told me that he wanted him to stay away from me, the shop, and the girls. Marky told me that his friend's heart was wicked. He was very protective of me and my girls.

I left Marky and the girls and went back to Canada to hustle more stock for the store and restaurant. I talked to Marky every night to find out how the store was going on and how he was doing. I also wanted to know if he was eating and if he had money. He was my concern. I had plans for him to improve his life because it was so easy for them to get into trouble, especially Marky; he was a 'hothead,' someone who easily reacted to anger. Some days he seemed lost and out of it; he was always thinking. I sensed that he did not know what to do with his life. It was Valentine's night and also Marky's birthday. I saw my phone ringing; it said Marky was calling but when I answered it was not Marky and my heart started beating faster.

I started asking, "Where is Marky? Let me speak to him. Please let me speak to Marky. I want to tell him Happy Birthday." On the other side of the phone, I heard, "Mama, you cannot speak to him." Now the tears started running down my eyes, "Please just tell Marky that I want to talk to him. I want to tell him that he will be coming to Canada soon." "Mami," the voice said from the other side of the phone, "He is dead." She told me that they shot Marky seven times in his head. I could never explain to this day the pain that I felt for Marky. His death really took a toll on me. I had to send money from the shop to bury him. At the funeral I spoke via my phone from Canada; I could not get any flights to go to Jamaica to his funeral because my travel documents were expired.

I eventually got my papers and returned to Jamaica, but it was another sad time for me just being in the country; Marky was not there. When I was in the house, I felt like his presence was around me. One night I dreamed that he was in the house wearing a white hat that I gave him. Marky, I wish they did not take him from me; he was like a son. I wish I could reverse time and things that happened. Until this day I miss him.

Chapter 17
The Last Hurrah

Marky's death caused me to introspect; it raised a lot of questions from within. Although we all have choices, some people only see one way out; they do not understand that we can choose how we want to live our lives especially when there is no one to mentor or give directions. I met a lot of people that lived in the ghetto and became successful, but it was not easy for them. There were nights without meals or sleeping in one-bedroom houses with the entire family. Some did not even get the chance to go to school but they survived and made it out. Then there are the weak ones who cannot see any other way out but the gangster life. I strongly believe that life takes you where you want it to.

I always heard the saying, "to be poor is a crime," and I have seen it played out in the lives of the young men that were protecting me; they were born into poverty. There were nights that they went to bed without food. As a child I experienced a little hunger. There was a period of food shortage in the village and even though mama and daddy had the food shop, they could not control the lack; the essential food like flour and rice were just not available.

Why?

As a child I did not eat ground provisions such as yam and banana; I guess those times we would call it poor people food and as a result of the shortage, after a while I knew what it felt like to be hungry. I will never forget how I felt like I was going to die, and my skin became pale. I quickly learned how delicious green bananas and yams were. In that moment of introspection, I asked myself, "why did I really gravitate to those young men; those gangsters, shotters and killers? Then I realized that it was not really because they were what they were, but it was their pain. I could identify with being rejected and hungry. I could feel their confusion and lack of love. I wanted to love and take care of them, but I could not manage, so I became like them. Marky wanted out and he was so excited when I told him that I wanted to take him to Canada to have a new life; now he was gone. He never got the opportunity that he dreamt of.

The Turning

After Marky's death, reality began to slowly kick in; I did not like my life anymore, I wanted out. I knew about God, but I did not have a relationship with him. I had Bible study sometimes in my store. There was a pastor that I had met in the plaza, Bishop Lazree Davis, he would come and pray with us in the shop. One of the cashiers was a Christian and sometimes I would wonder how she managed being around us, around me and all the gangsters coming to the store. She was always smiling, the guys respected her, and they never tried to hit on her. One day while I was at the store, a customer invited me to the universal church; I went one afternoon, and I saw a lot of stores and business owners fellowshipping.

There was something that I did not understand about that church hence I did not go there for long, but I knew there was a part of me that always needed God and it was time. I needed to get my home and my life in order. I was wrestling with two angels; one wanted to do good but evil kept presenting itself. There was a tug of war going on within me, but it seemed as though evil was winning. The battle was raging, and I left for Canada.

Plan Gone Wrong

They say early birds catch the most worms and four of us decided to roll that early morning. First stop was the Outlets. We split up, and two of us went to the Men's Warehouse. The stores were practically empty with only a cashier busy doing paperwork; hence we pulled out the garbage bags and began to pack them fast. We brought out the first set of bags to the cars and decided we wanted to go back again; my partner went to another store. While I was in the store packing my bags, customers started coming in and I had to hide the bags. After hiding the bags, I began looking around for an escape route then I looked up at the entrance and could not believe my eyes; two police officers were standing there looking around. Then I saw another policeman going into the car with my friend. Immediately I moved towards the back of the store trying to figure out what to do.

I looked around to see if there was anyone watching me trying to open the back door to go through but there was another door with an alarm on it. I felt trapped when I saw the policemen walking around the store and heading towards the back, but I was already determined that I was not going to jail. I also prayed that my partner did not call my name. I wondered if the policemen thought that there was another accomplice because they knew that we walked in pairs. I saw them but they did not see me, so I grabbed a hat off the store shelf and some clothes off the rack and ran into the change room. I changed my clothes, took off my wig and boosted it between my legs then I threw the clothes that I had on under a rack where they could not be seen. I quickly came out of the changing room to prevent anyone seeing me leaving without clothes in hand.

The police were at the back of the store talking to one of the workers who seemed like he had just come into work hence I moved towards the front, grabbed a top off the rack and went to the cashier to make my purchase. The police came down to the front and started looking at me. At that time my phone rang, and I answered it in African gibberish. The truth was I did not know how to speak any other language but English and patois, but I pretended as though I was speaking African. The police asked me if I was shopping alone but I pretended that I did not understand English, so I kept asking them "police me in trouble? " I continued, "Oh no, me? No problem, love Canada." Then one of the police said, "No trouble, no trouble."

I heard the police asking the cashier if there was any other customer in the store. She told him no and they left. I saw the police driving away with my partner and my other friends drove away with the van and left me stranded. We always planned ahead of time that if anything happened to any of us, for example if we got caught, someone would get the goods away from the scene.

I had to find my way home and I did it as quickly as I could. On my way, my friends and I met at a restaurant and talked about what happened. We also waited to hear what happened to our other friend because she was an illegal immigrant in Canada. I felt horrible because I was the one that taught her how to boost and after that she wanted to go out with us every day. While talking, we met the owner of the restaurant and he perceived that we were bad girls; I guess he heard us talking about the police, so he started a conversation with me about God. He tried inviting us to his church, but we did not have church on our minds. However, I promised him that one day I would be there; he gave me his number just in case I needed it.

Breaking Protocol

We finally got news about our friend, she got out because she did not have any record, so the police gave her a chance. I guess the police did not find out that she was illegal. We were all packing to return to Jamaica; the barrels were all set. Now there was no one in the house in Jamaica; Shawty and I broke up and I got myself a baby boy from the Monster Crew. My girlfriend said I was a cradle robber, but I told her I was a cougar; it was all about Gangsta and Monster. Now, do not let the name fool you; the Monster Crew was packed with all cuties. The word quickly got out on the street that I was dating Rashad Monster but the Gangsters around me did not like the idea that I was with another man from another area. In Jamaica, they were big on areas; certain sections were not allowed to cross other territories or lives would be lost; I was breaking protocol. I arrived in Jamaica on a late flight, and I wanted Rashad to come to the house; I wanted to see my baby. I called him as soon as I arrived at my house, and it did not take long for him to get there. I could see the faces of the other men in the house, they were making serious faces at him like, "Who does this Nigga think he is?" I tried to bring some good vibes in the house, but it was hard for him to be in the same environment around so many shotters. We survived the night, but it was obvious that it would be a bumpy ride.

It was Christmas time, and it was pretty busy for the store, but the girls were there to help. I also started hanging out in Rashad's neighborhood which drew a lot of attention. He was from Rocky Point, a place where people from all over the world would travel desiring to buy fish and also party. I love fish, especially Panga, so he always ensured that his mom cooked it for me. I could see the look on his face when we were together; it was like I cannot believe that I am with this woman. It was though he caught a big fish. When a "stallion" a younger man dated an older woman with money and owned a business they called her "The Real Big Woman'. Well, that was what I was to Rashad. However, it was not long until I heard that they were planning to kill him. There was a lot of jealousy, they hated him which made me worried. Hence, I stopped him from coming to my house.

However, our relationship had not ended, therefore, I moved some of my clothes to his room where he was living. One night we were lying in his room when he heard gunshots blazing on the road. The next day some guys came to Rashad's room and told him that the gunfire was from the shotters that hang around me. They told him that he had to be careful because they wanted to kill him. I did not want Rashad to die so I moved back to my house.

My Don

My Don called me and told me to give Shawty a chance. Everyone wanted us to get back together but I could not, my heart was not there anymore. That night we went to a party, Shawty, the crew and I. While we partied with some of Dancehall's popular artists who respected my Don, I could see on everybody's face that they were all happy to see Shawty and I back together again or that was how it seemed. We were all drinking hard and partying like crazy. I kept looking at my Don and my secret inner feelings resurfaced; I wished he was my man. He attracted people to him wherever we went. However, I never told him how I felt because I loved the friendship that we had and plus, he used to have a relationship with my friend. The woman that he was with at the time also became a good friend of mine, so I just kept my cool.

That night, I took the microphone while the music was playing. I asked the DJ to lower the music and I announced to the entire dance that he was my God; yeah, my Don was my God. After I made that announcement something inside me changed; no one knew what was happening to me. It felt like the alcohol left my body; I did not feel drunk anymore. I told the guys that I wanted to leave, and everyone was saying, "Gee, the party just started, you cannot leave now." I wanted to leave, and Shawty was getting upset. I saw my Don looking at me, but I had to leave. I got home that morning feeling really awful about what I had done. As a young girl we were taught that there was only one God and that was the Creator of the world. Even though I was drunk I knew what I was doing because it did not feel right; I knew something was wrong with me, my daughters even told me that some of my features had changed.

They seemed worried and wanted to go back to Canada. It was almost like I was possessed with a spirit called "Gangsta." I spoke to my daughters harshly. I remember Tayshean's dad came to visit me, and he acted as if he were looking at a totally different person when he saw me; that was weird because he was a real G.

The Bombshell

The people that I looked to and trusted suddenly started going against me. Chef was one of my inner circle guys, he took care of my business, and he ran the restaurant that I had opened at that time. He was my right hand; he kept me updated on what was happening when I was otherwise occupied. He was also jealous of certain people that came around me. He was especially angry when I started dating Rashad, so he started talking behind my back and also tried turning my Don against me. I do not know what he told him, but it caused him to come to my home with a gun.

One morning I was in bed sleeping when I was awakened by a knock on the grill. It was like someone was using a gun or something to draw on the grill; I could hear the noise going back and forth. When I went to the grill I saw Daddy, the name I sometimes called my Don. I ran towards the grill to open it but instead of a smile, I ran to a gun pointing right at my face. He seemed so angry that morning, I could see it in his eyes. "Hey gal, you want me to shoot you in your face?"

he said. I did not know what to say because right there my entire world crumbled. He then told me not to call his name and to stay away from him. Daddy walked away from the grill, but I was still standing there in tears.

I want Out

My Sunday morning routine included the playing of gospel music, so I started playing a song by Jabez. However, that could not stop the tears; I cried so hard that I wanted to return to Canada right away. I knew that my time in Jamaica was up. I did not think that I could make it in Jamaica with my Don not wanting me around him. He never told me why he was so angry that he pointed a gun in my face, so I wanted out of the game. I felt like my time was coming; like it was my turn to die. One morning, before going back to Canada, I left the shop and went to Miracle Faith Temple for fasting service; I spent the entire day there singing and praying. I remember being at the altar and hearing an inner voice saying, "your name will change from Gangsta to Warrior." I got up from the altar and there was my friend Jelissa, she was wearing a skimpy top and tights. She wanted to know why I was hanging out in the church so long. She said she was at the shop waiting for me then she decided to come to the church. I told her, "I want to change my life." However, Jelissa was not interested in hearing that because her hype had just started.

She loved when we partied together; she loved the hype. That day at the church, I felt that the Lord was calling me, but I was not completely ready. I did not know how to walk away from the lifestyle that I was living. I wanted to give up the shop and to get rid of everything. The word circulated that I was changing my life, and everyone came to my house for my clothes.

Do not Do It

I wanted a new life! I was empty and hurt. Most of the men around me disappeared; they were either in jail or dead. Jamaica became unbearable. Subsequently, I booked an early ticket and went back to Canada. My birthday week was coming up and I planned to attend a big dance. I got an absolutely gorgeous, tailored dress and a beautiful name brand Gwen Stafane shoes and my lace-front wig was rocking. I would like to talk about that night but…we did not party for a long time in T-Dot (Toronto).

The day before the party Lisa, the Christian cashier at my shop in Jamaica, kept calling me but I did not answer her; she was always telling me that God was calling me. My workers were loyal to me. Even if they were discussing my behavior, they would never tell me; I guess they loved their jobs. When I finally answered my phone, she told me that she had a dream that my shoes were bundled up under a tree. I did not know what that meant but she told me not to go to any party. However, I was just thinking that Lisa was telling me all those things because she wanted me to change my life; therefore, I totally ignored her. Nothing and no one could have stopped me from going to that party especially on my birth night.

She Died

My birth night was supposed to be glamorous, but that night Yvonne Gangsta died on the dance floor. Later, Yvonne Reid, the new me, woke up in North York General Hospital to the ligaments in my feet not only torn but unable to be restored. I was told that I would not walk normally again, and surgery was needed to stop the flow of fluid building in my knee. To add insult to injury there were those so-called friends that only visited to collect a report for others; that really hurt. However, I was even more saddened because my loved ones were not yet at the hospital. In the end my mother had to learn about the tragedy on the news. Later my son came to the hospital. After a thorough examination, I got discharged the following Saturday.

After I arrived home, gangsters came in droves and I knew what that meant. Coupled with the numerous phone calls from Jamaica, America, and the news that my attackers were going on a cruise, I knew things were about to get really ugly; I knew I had to think quickly. While thinking, I felt peace, retaliating was not the answer; lives would have been lost on both sides. I just did not want to do anything, and I surely did not want any more death, I just did not want it. I told my men that I was finished with that lifestyle, that I did not want any more war. I did not want any more deaths and my time was up.

Gangsta died that night in the club; that was where she was born and that was where I had to leave her. On July 4, 2010, the devil came in for the kill, but God said, "You are no longer Gangsta, you shall be called Warrior. Gangsta had to die in order for Yvonne to live...

The Road to Recovery

For many months, I was in excruciating pain, but I was determined to defy the odds and walk again. The police came and took pictures of my bruised body- it was difficult. A few days later, I went to the clinic and did an X-ray in preparation for my surgery. While there, the neurologist said, "it is going to be a very difficult surgery hence it is best to watch the knee to see if the swelling will go down. Therefore, take this medication and return in a few weeks." The time came and I went back to the doctor. Surprisingly the surgery was cancelled, and he recommended doing therapy first. That night my world came crashing down and I started praying to God and asking Him to help me; I felt so lonely. My gangsters, "my friends" no longer came to visit me.

The road to recovery brought much emotional pain as people on the street were celebrating my downfall but it also reminded me of the harsh reality that I should have died.

I remember one day the chicken vendor from the dance came to visit and share with me what really happened that night. He said gunshots rained like cats and dogs; he thought that I died. He also said he had to visit to encourage me to walk away from that lifestyle or I was going to lose my life. Based on the incident some people said someone tried to witchcraft me, but I believe that God was calling me. I know that God would not harm me, but he would allow things to happen as a wakeup call. I woke up.

Chapter 18
I Woke Up

After Gangsta died, reality check in and I had to start my life all over. It took a few months to physically recover from my assault. I spent a lot of time at home until I was super bored of home. My foot was still swollen and extremely painful when I decided to go back to college. My desire was always to go back to Bible College and finish what I started. I remember going to a Bible College down on Keele Street to speak to the administration about signing up for the fall class. She however suggested that I first pursue acquiring my grade twelve school leaving certificate. I was somewhat disappointed because I wanted to do something. I wasn't used to staying at home. I took her advice and registered at Centennial College and after one year of studies, I successfully graduated with my grade twelve certificate.

Let me remind you that all those times I didn't hear from my so-called friends. This was a dreadful time in my life. I painfully learned that when you are at your lowest that's when you will know who is with you and who is not. The truth of the matter was no one was with me. I was at home alone...

I was then a grade twelve graduate and now asking myself what I should do with my life. I wanted to study social work, but I had a criminal record and was rejected from pursuing that ambition. Additionally, student loans denied my application citing I was in arrears with them.

Therefore, I went to God about it. "Dear God, where is it that you want me to go?"

THE DREAM

I went to my bed and dreamt that I was in a woman's house searching for her. This dream was so real. In the dream I could not find her. This lady was someone I knew many years before. Both her and her husband were the assistant pastors at my church. I had not been to church for many years and now I was dreaming about her. Interestingly, in the dream I couldn't find her. At one point in the dream, I was in her library, and I saw her grandson in the room. I asked him, "where is your grandmother", and he pointed his finger outside of the room and I woke up. I didn't understand the dream, so I called Ma who was one of the mothers in the church that took care of the newcomers and visitors as they came into the church. I haven't spoken to Ma for many years as well. I never kept in touch. I was a backslider, and I chose to stay away. I told her about the dream. She was rather surprised to hear from me and even more surprised about the dream. She said, "Yvonne the Lord is calling you to go to Bible College," Well why would she say that" I thought. Ma said the lady in the dream was working at the Bible college. She sent me to Canada Christian College to find the missing lady in my dream. I found Carmen Delzoto the missing lady and that year I registered at the college and became a student.

My life completely turned around. I became a member of Faith Miracle Temple where I was on their committee board planning events which was very successful. I graduated from Bible College with my Bachelor of Theology and Master's in Divinity. I also work at the college as a Maintenance Manager and Call Center Supervisor. After seven years at the college, I went into becoming a Child and Youth Care Worker. Now I had to work for my money, and it felt good. I didn't have to look over my shoulder anymore. I spent many years in that field of helping children with challenges. Within that time, I became a member of Scarborough Church of God where I became the leader of the Evangelism Department. Later on, I moved to starting my own online church, The Love Church (TLC) which is very impactful.

God preserved and rescued me from self-destruct and the many devices of the enemy that I chased aggressively. Today I am an ambassador for the Most High God. Jesus is my savior and has made everything new in me. I am a new creation.

<u>I am no longer Gangsta, I am Warrior.</u>

Conclusion

'Big up my Don, He is my God'. The Bible says, 'Thou shall have no other Gods before Him,' (Exodus 20:3) the Creator. The kingdom of God is accessible to all, even those who believe they are the greatest sinners and have totally lost their way from God's path. He will leave the ninety-nine to come looking for you and He will not stop until he finds you because you belong to Him. The God who saved Gangsta is also able to do the same for you.

About the Author

Yvonne Reid is Jamaican born and currently reside in Toronto Canada. She is the executive pastor of The Love Church-an online church through the Caribbean and North America. She is a graduate of Canada Christian College, with a Master's in divinity in theology with an emphasis on Evangelism and Christian Counselling. Yvonne not only brings these achievements to the table, but also builds her table as the proud mother of five beautiful children and 6 adorable grandchildren.

Yvonne inspiration to write this book comes from a desire to giving hope. That it doesn't matter what challenges we have faced in life.

Either we allow it to keep us down or keep us moving.

Yvonne can be reached at reidyvonne@gmail.com

www.ingramcontent.com/pod-product-compliance
Lightning Source LLC
Chambersburg PA
CBHW050252010526
44107CB00003B/289